# Basics of Web Technologies

## ABOUT THE AUTHORS

**Mr. Dumpa Sreepal** is an Assistant Professor at Loyola Academy Degree and P.G College Hyderabad. He holds multiple postgraduate degrees including MCA, MBA, MA, M.Sc. (Maths). He is currently pursuing a Ph.D. in Mathematics from RTMNU (Nagpur state University)

Mr. Sreepal has over 12 years of teaching experience, with expertise spanning both technical and management subjects. He has authored several research articles published in reputed national and international journals. His areas of interest are Mathematics, Management, and Technical research, and he actively contributes to academic literature in these fields. In addition to his publications, he also holds two patents, reflecting his innovative contributions to academia and applied research.

**Dr. L Madan Mohan** is an Incharge principal at Aditya Group of Colleges (Formerly Mother Teresa Group of Institutions), his qualifications are MCA MTech MBA PhD and currently pursuing PhD in computers. He did his Doctoral Thesis on "A study on Brand Awareness with reference to Hyderabad Region" from RTMNU Nagpur and has 18 years' experience in both computer science and management courses. he has published a book on data communication and computer networks and several articles in national and international journals with Scopus indexing also. he has 2 patents and copyright to his name.

**Ms. Chittimilla Bhavana** is a faculty member at Loyola Academy, Suchitra, Hyderabad. She holds a postgraduate degree, M.Sc. in Computer Science. She is dedicated to teaching Computer Science subjects and guiding students in both theoretical and practical aspects of learning. Her academic interests include Programming, Data Analytics, and Database Management Systems. She actively participates in academic activities and strives to enhance students' technical and problem-solving skills.

**Mrs. Palaparthi Shailaja** is an Associate Professor at Vishwa Vishwani Institute of Systems and Management. She holds dual postgraduate degrees in MCA and M.Tech (Computer Science). With over 20 years of teaching experience in postgraduate and undergraduate colleges, along with 10 years of teaching experience in various high schools, she has made significant contributions to education. She has authored multiple course contents for postgraduate students and has actively participated in various academic workshops and professional development programs.

# Basics of
# WEB TECHNOLOGIES

Mr. Dumpa Sreepal
Dr. L Madan Mohan,
Ms. Chittimilla Bhavana
Mrs. Palaparthi Shailaj

ACADEMIC
ENCLAVE

*First Edition, 2026*

ISBN: 978-93-48642-05-9

*Published by*
**ACADEMIC ENCLAVE™**
House No. 10/15, Ground Floor,
Block-A, Street No. 14/3, Kamal Vihar,
Kamal Pur, Burari, Delhi-110084
*Email: info@academicenclave.com*
*Mobile: +91-7042423166*
*Website: www.academicenclave.com*

# Preface

The rapid growth of the Internet and web-based applications has transformed the way people communicate, learn, and conduct business. Web Technologies play a vital role in developing interactive, dynamic, and user-friendly websites and web applications. A strong understanding of these technologies is essential for students pursuing Computer Science, Information Technology, Data Science, Artificial Intelligence, and related disciplines.

This book has been carefully prepared according to the latest undergraduate syllabus. It provides a clear and systematic introduction to the fundamental concepts of Web Technologies, beginning with the World Wide Web, web browsers, web servers, HTTP, and HTML5. The book gradually progresses to advanced topics such as CSS3, JavaScript, XML, PHP, and database connectivity using MySQL.

Each chapter is presented in a simple and easy-to-understand manner with well-structured explanations, definitions, syntax, examples, diagrams, and practical programs. Real-world examples and hands-on coding exercises have been included to help students understand both theoretical concepts and practical implementation.

The primary objective of this book is to build a strong foundation in web development while enabling students to design and develop responsive and interactive web applications. It is intended to serve as a valuable resource for undergraduate students, faculty members, and beginners who wish to learn modern web technologies.

Every effort has been made to ensure the accuracy and clarity of the content. Suggestions and constructive feedback from readers and educators are always welcome and will help improve future editions of this book.

I sincerely hope that this book will serve as a useful learning companion and inspire students to explore the exciting field of web development with confidence.

**Mr. Dumpa Sreepal**

**Dr. L Madan Mohan**

**Ms. Chittimilla Bhavana**

**Mrs. Palaparthi Shailaj**

# Syllabus

## Module I: Introduction to World Wide Web

Web Browsers, Web Servers, DOM, HTTP, HTML, HTML5, Structure of HTML page, HTML5 Tags, Links, Input, Images, Favicon, Lists.

## Module II:

HTML Tables, Creating Forms, Html audio, Html Media, Styling Forms, Placeholder, Inline and Block elements, Id vs Class elements.

## Module III:

CSS3-Basics, CSS3 Syntax, Comments, Including CSS3 in HTML Documents, CSS3-Selectors: Universal Selector, Element Type Selector, Id Selectors, Class Selectors, Group Selectors, CSS3-Styles: CSS Color, CSS Background, CSS Fonts, CSSText, CSS Links, CSS Lists, CSS Tables

## Module IV:

CSS3 - Box Model: Margin, Padding, Border, Outline, Visibility, Display, Multiple Columns, JavaScript: Introduction to JavaScript, Java Script and Forms Variables, Functions, Operators, Conditional Statements and Loops.

## Module V:

Arrays, DOM Methods, Strings, Dialogue Boxes-Alert, Confirmation, prompt Box. Events Handling, Introduction to XML: XML basics, Structuring data, Document type definition and its types, XML Namespaces, XML DOM.

## Module VI: Overview Of PHP

General Syntactic Characteristics Primitives, Operations and Expressions Output, Control Statements, Arrays, Functions Pattern Matching, Form Handling, Files, Cookies and Session Tracking Database access through web: Architectures for database access My SQL Database System, Database access with PHP and My SQL

# Contents

# Module: I

# Introduction to World Wide Web

## 1.1 Web Browsers, Web Servers, DOM, HTTP

### Web Browser

It is one of the most important components of the World Wide Web. Whenever we want to access any website, the first tool we use is a web browser.

A web browser acts as a bridge between the user and the internet.

It allows users to request web pages and display them in a readable format.

It is essential for accessing and interacting with web content.

#### ▶ Definition

A web browser can be defined as a software application that is used to retrieve, understand and display web pages from the internet. It takes the content received from the web server and converts it into a visual format that users can understand.

#### ▶ Working of Web Browser

When a user enters a website address in the browser, the browser sends a request to the web server using HTTP.

The server processes the request and sends back the web page.

The browser then reads the HTML structure, applies CSS styles and executes JavaScript code.

Finally, it displays the web page on the screen.

User
↓
Enter URL
↓
Browser Request
↓
Web Server
↓
Response
↓
Browser Display

**Fig 1.1: Working of Web Browser**

**Examples:** Google Chrome, Mozilla Firefox, Microsoft Edge and Safari.

### ▶ Features of Web Browser

1. It allows navigation between pages using links.
2. It supports multimedia content such as images and videos.
3. It provides security features such as private browsing.
4. It also supports extensions and tools that enhance user experience.

## 1.2 Web Server

When a user accesses a website using a web browser, the content of that website must come from somewhere. This content is stored and provided by a web server.

### ▶ Definition

A web server can be defined as a system or software that stores web pages and delivers them to users over the internet when requested.It receives requests from web browsers and sends back the required web pages using HTTP protocol.

### ▶ Working of Web Server

1. When a user enters a website address in the browser, the browser sends a request to the web server.
2. The server receives this request, processes it and sends back the suitable response in the form of a web page.
3. The browser then displays this web page to the user.

User
↓
Browser
↓
Request
↓
Web Server
↓
Process
↓
Response
↓
Browser
↓
Display

**Fig 1.2: Working of Web Server**

### ▶ Functions of Web Server

1. It stores website files such as HTML, CSS and images.
2. It processes user requests and sends appropriate responses.
3. It also manages multiple users accessing the server at the same time.
4. The web server ensures smooth communication between users and web content.

## 1.3 DOM (Document Object Model)

When a web page is loaded in a browser, it is not directly treated as plain text.

Instead, the browser converts the entire HTML document into a structured format that can be easily accessed and modified.

This structured representation of the web page is called the DOM.

DOM acts as a bridge between the web page and programming languages such as JavaScript.

DOM is used to create dynamic web content or web page. When the user runs the HTML documents, the DOM object is created and designs the page dynamic.

DOM is present at server side.

The Document Object Model can be defined as a tree-like structure that represents the elements of an HTML document as objects. Each part of the web page, such as headings, paragraphs and images, is treated as a node in this structure.

### ▶ Structure of DOM

The DOM represents the HTML document in the form of a hierarchical tree.

The entire document is considered as the root, and each element is connected as parent and child nodes.

For example, the HTML element is the root, which contains the head and body elements.

The body further contains elements such as paragraphs, images and links.

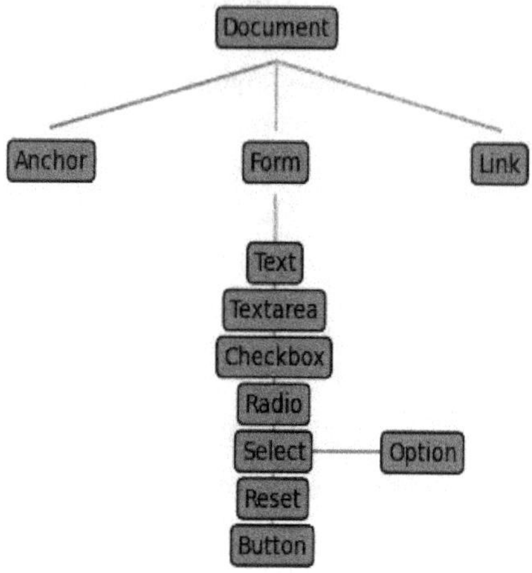


**Fig 1.1: DOM Tree Structure**

- **Methods:**
  1. **write():** It return the string
  2. **writeln():**It return the string to the new line.
  3. **getElementById():**It return the element with specific ID.
  4. **getElementByTagName():** It returns the count of the tags names used in the HTML document.
  5. **getElementByName():** It returns the count of the name used inthe HTML document.

- **Working of DOM**
  1. When a web page is loaded, the browser creates the DOM structure. This structure can then be accessed using JavaScript.
  2. Using DOM, we can change the content, style and structure of the web page dynamically.
  3. In real-world usage, suppose a web page contains a paragraph. Using JavaScript and DOM, we can change the text of that paragraph when a button is clicked.
  4. For example:

     Initial text: "Hello"

     After click: "Welcome"

## 1.4 HTTP (Hyper Text Transfer Protocol)

It is a protocol used for transferring data between a web-browser(client) and a web server.

It is a stateless protocol which is used to communicate information between clients and servers.

It is the foundation of communication on the World Wide Web.

It is also known as Request-Response Model.

It consists of following stages:

1. **Connection**: The clint establishes a connection with web server.
2. **Request**: The client sends a request message to web server.
3. **Response**: The web server sends the response.
4. **Close**: The connection is closed by web server.

### ▶ Working of HTTP

1. When a user enters a website address in the browser, the browser sends an HTTP request to the web server.
2. The server receives this request, processes it and sends back an HTTP response containing the requested data.
3. The browser then displays this data in the form of a web page.

Client (Browser) → HTTP Request → Server → HTTP Response → Client → Display

### ▶ Types of HTTP Messages

#### 1. HTTP Request Format:

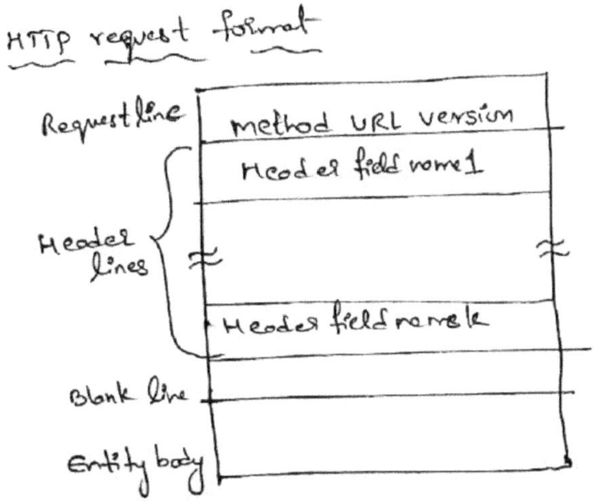


**Fig 1.2: HTTP Request Response**

The first line of a HTTP request message is called the request line.

The following lines are called header lines till a blank line.

The requested line has three fields separated by a space.

There are few HTTP request methods such as GET, POST, PUT, HEAD, DELETE, OPTIONS.

2. **HTTP Response Format:**

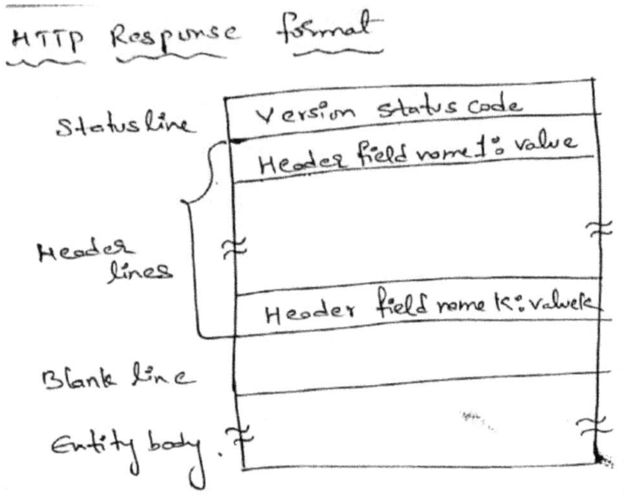


**Fig 1.3: HTTP Response Format**

The first line of HTTP response message is called status line.

The blank line does not store anything hence it is blank or empty.

The following lines till the blank line are called header lines.

The entity body contains requested object itself.

The status line has three fields separated by space.

### ▶ Example

For example, when a user types a website URL in the browser:

The browser sends an HTTP request to the server and server processes the request.

The server sends back the web page as a response

The browser displays the page

### ▶ Features of HTTP

1. HTTP is a stateless protocol, which means each request is independent and does not remember previous requests.
2. It is simple and flexible.

3. It is suitable for transferring different types of data.
4. HTTP is widely used for web communication.

## 1.5 Origin and Evolution of HTML

- In 1989, Tim Berners invented WWW.
- In 1991, Tim Berners-Lee invented first version of HTML (HTML 1.0).
- In 1993, Dave Raggett drafted HTML+.
- In 1995, Tim Berners along with Dave Raggett worked on HTML and defined HTML 2 .0.
- In 1997, W3C recommended 3.2 HTML version.
- In 1999, W3C recommended HTML 4.0 version.
- In 2000, XHTML 1.0 version was recommended by W3C.
- In 2008, $5^{th}$ version of HTML was invented which was known as HTML5.
- The current version of HTML is 5.1 ($2^{nd}$ edition).

## 1.6 HTML5: Introduction, Structure of HTML Page

### Introduction

HTML5 is the foundation of web page development. HTML stands for HyperText Markup Language, and it is used to create the structure of web pages.

Every website that we see on the internet is built using HTML in combination with other technologies such as CSS and JavaScript.

Over a period of time, HTML has evolved, and the latest version is HTML5.

HTML5 is used to define the structure of a web page, while CSS is used for styling and JavaScript is used for interactivity.

- **Definition:** HTML5 can be defined as the latest version of HyperText Markup Language used to create and structure content on the web. It allows developers to define elements such as headings, paragraphs, images, links and multimedia content in a web page.

### Features of HTML5

1. It supports audio and video elements without the need for external plugins.
2. It introduces new semantic tags that improve the structure of web pages.
3. It also supports graphics, forms and improved user interaction.
4. HTML5 enhances both functionality and user experience.

**Structure of HTML Page**: An HTML page follows a standard structure that helps the browser to understand and display the content properly.

### ▶ Basic Structure of HTML Page

An HTML document is made up of different elements arranged in a specific order. The main parts of an HTML page are:

1. Document declaration
2. HTML element
3. Head section
4. Body section

### ▶ Structure of HTML Page

```
<!DOCTYPE html>
<html>
<head>
<title></title>
</head>
<body>
</body>
</html>
```

**1. Document Declaration (<!DOCTYPE html>):** The document declaration is written at the beginning of the HTML file. It tells the browser that the document is written in HTML 5. It helps the browser to interpret the page correctly.

**2. HTML Tag (<html>):** The HTML tag is the root element of the web page. It contains all the other elements of the document. Everything inside the page is enclosed within the HTML tag.<html> is the root tag or parent tag and represents the starting of the HTML code.

**3. Head Section (<head>):** The head section contains information about the web page, such as title and metadata. It does not display content directly on the page but provides information to the browser. It helps in defining page properties.<head> tag is the sub element or meta element of information of HTML. It is a container for metadata (data about data) and is placed between <html> tag and <body> tag.

**4. Body Section (<body>):** The body section contains the actual content of the web page that is visible to the user. It includes elements such as headings, paragraphs, images and links.

### ▶ Example Code:

```
<!DOCTYPE html>
<html>
<head>
```

```
<title>My First WT Program</title>
</head>
<body>
<h1>Welcome</h1>
<p>This is a HTML Program</p>
</body>
</html>
```

Output:

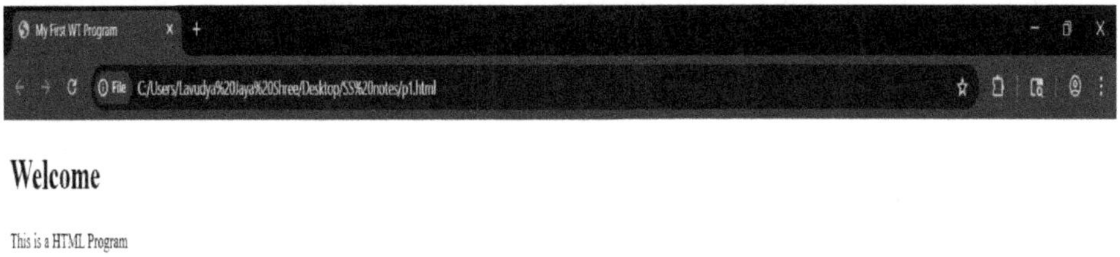


### ▶ Importance of HTML Structure

1. The structure of an HTML page is important because it ensures proper organization of content.
2. It also improves readability and maintainability of the code.
3. A well-structured HTML page is easy to develop and understand.

## 1.7 HTML5 Tags, Links, Input, Images, Favicon, Lists

### HTML5 Tags

HTML5 tags are the basic building blocks of any web page. In HTML, content is not written as plain text, but it is enclosed within special keywords called tags. These tags tell the browser how to display the content on the web page. Without tags, the browser will not understand how to structure or present the content.

### ▶ Definition

HTML5 tags can be defined as predefined keywords used to create and structure content in a web page. These tags are written inside angle brackets (<>) and usually come in pairs, consisting of an opening tag and a closing tag.

### ▶ Structure of a Tag

A typical HTML tag consists of:

1. Opening tag
2. Content
3. Closing tag

```
<opentag>content</closetag>
```

For example:

<p> This is a paragraph </p>

Here, <p> is the opening tag and </p> is the closing tag.

## ▶ Types of HTML5 Tags

There are N number of predefined tags which are used in HTML programming

1. <html> is a root tag or parent Tag and represent starting of the HTML code
2. <head> tag is a sub element or meta data (data about data) of Information of HTML and it is placed between <html> tag and <body> tag. However, it is not mandatory to write in a program.
3. <title> tag represents the title of the page
4. <body> tag defines a document and it is a container for all visible contents such as heading paragraph images tables list hyperlink etc.
5. Heading Tags (<h1> to <h6>) are used to define headings in a web page. It represents one or more heading elements i.e., there are six levels of headings from <h1> to <h6>, where <h1> is the largest and <h6> is the smallest. These are titles or subtitles that you want to display on a web page.

For example,

```
<!DOCTYPE html>
<html>
<body>
<h1>Welcome 1</h1>
<h2>Welcome 2</h2>
<h3>Welcome 3</h3>
<h4>Welcome 4</h4>
<h5>Welcome 5</h5>
<h6>Welcome 6</h6>
</body>
</html>
```

Output:

# Welcome 1

## Welcome 2

### Welcome 3

#### Welcome 4

##### Welcome 5

###### Welcome 6

1. <p> tagdefines a paragraph. It is one of the most commonly used tags in HTML.
2. <br> stands for break and used a break a line in paragraph.
3. Formatting tags are used to style text. For example:
    - <b> for bold text
    - <i> for italic text
    - <strong> for important text.
    - <em> emphasised text
    - <mark> used to mark any text
    - <small> used to represent small text
    - <del> used to delete any text
    - <ins> used to insert any text
    - <sub> subscript tag
    - <sup> superscript tag

For example,

```
<!DOCTYPE html>
<html>
<title> formatting tags </title>
<body>
<p><b> for bold text </b></p>
<p><i> for italic text </i></p>
<p>for <strong>important</strong> text </p>
<p><em> emphasised text </em></p>
<p><mark> used to mark </mark> any text</p>
<p><small> used to represent small text </small></p>
```

```
<p><del> used </del> to delete any text</p>
<p>used to <ins> insert </ins> any text</p>
<p><sub> subscript tag </sub></p>
<p><sup> superscript tag </sup></p>
</body>
</html>
```

1. Semantic tags such as <header>, <footer>, <section> and <article>. These tags describe the meaning of the content. Semantic tags improve readability and structure.
2. Multimedia tags such as <audio> and <video> to include multimedia content directly in web pages.
3. <a> anchor tag is used to create hyperlinks that connect one page to another.

## HTML Links

The web is called a "web" because different web pages are connected to each other through links. Links allow users to navigate from one page to another or from one website to another. Without links, browsing the internet would not be possible.

### ▶ Definition

An HTML link can be defined as an element that is used to connect one web page to another. It is created using the anchor tag <a>.

Links are created using anchor tags.

### ▶ Structure of a Link

A link consists of anchor tag <a>, attribute href (Hyper Text Reference) and link text.

For example:

```
<a href="https://example.com">Visit Website</a>
```

href specifies the destination of the link.

### ▶ Types of Links

**1. External Links:** External links connect to another website.

Example:

```
<a href="https://example.com">Open Website</a>
```

They are used to navigate outside the current site.

**2. Internal Links**: Internal links connect to another page within the same website.

Example:

```
<a href="about.html">About Page</a>
```

They help in navigation within the website.

**3. Anchor Links**: Anchor links are used to navigate within the same page.

Example:

```
<a href="#section1">Go to Section</a>
```

They are used for page navigation.

### ▶ Attributes of Link

1. **href**: specifies the URL
2. **target**: specifies where to open the link

Example:

```
<a href="https://example.com" target="_blank">Open</a>
```

Attributes control link behavior.

### ▶ Example Code

```
<!DOCTYPE html>
<html>
<body>
<a href="https://example.com">Visit Website</a>
</body>
</html>
```

## HTML Input (Forms)

Input in HTML, which is used to collect data from users.

In many web applications such as login pages, registration forms and search bars, users are required to enter information. This interaction is made possible using input elements in HTML forms.

Input fields allow communication between the user and the web application.

### ▶ Definition

An HTML input element can be defined as a form control used to accept data from the user. It is created using the <input> tag. Input elements help in collecting user information.

A form is a container that holds input elements such as text boxes, buttons and checkboxes. It is created using the <form> tag. Forms group multiple input elements together.

### ▶ Types of Input Fields

**1. Text Input**: used to enter plain text such as name.

Example: <input type="text">

**2. Password Input**: used to enter passwords where characters are hidden.

Example: <input type="password">

**3. Email Input:** used to enter email addresses with validation.

Example: <input type="email">

**4. Number Input:** used to enter numeric values.

Example: <input type="number">

**5. Radio Button:** used to select one option from multiple choices.

Example: <input type="radio">

**6. Checkbox:** used to select multiple options.

Example: <input type="checkbox">

**7. Submit Button:** used to submit the form data.

Example: <input type="submit">

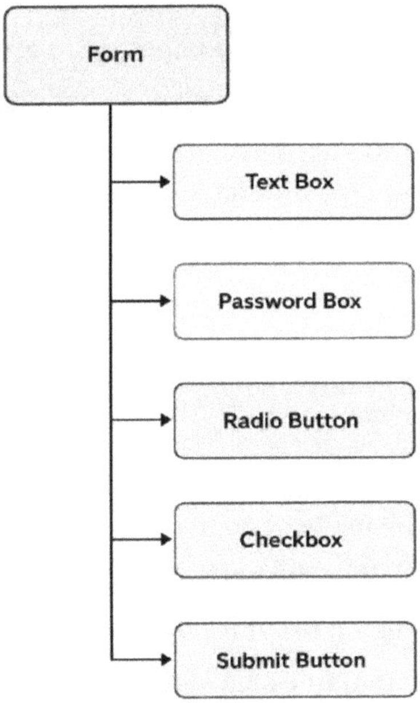


**Fig 1.3: Structure of HTML Form**

**Example:**

```
<!DOCTYPE html>
<html>
<body>
<form>
   Name: <input type="text"><br>
   Password: <input type="password"><br>
   Gender: <input type="radio"> Male
<input type="radio"> Female<br>
<input type="submit" value="Submit">
</form>
</body>
</html>
```

## HTML Images

Images in HTML are used to make web pages more attractive and informative.

Images help in presenting information visually and improve user experience.

In practical usage, images are used in websites for logos, banners, product images and icons.For example, an e-commerce website displays product images to help users understand the product better.

### ▶ Definition

An image in HTML can be defined as a graphical element that is displayed on a web page using the <img> tag.This tag is used to embed images such as photos, icons and graphics into a web page.

### ▶ Structure of Image Tag

The <img> tag is a self-closing tag and mainly uses attributes such as:

1. **src (source)**: specifies the path of the image
2. **alt (alternative text)**: provides description of the image
3. **width and height**: define size of the image

Example:

```
<imgsrc="image. jpg" alt="description" width="size">
```

Attributes define how the image is displayed.

### ▶ Working of Images

1. When the browser reads the <img> tag, it looks for the image file specified in the src attribute.
2. It then loads and displays the image on the web page.
3. If the image is not found, the text given in the alt attribute is displayed.

The browser fetches and displays images.

### ▶ Example

```
<!DOCTYPE html>
<html>
<body>
<h1>My Image</h1>
<imgsrc="photo.jpg" alt="My Photo" width="300">
</body>
</html>
```

### ▶ Types of Images Paths

#### 1. Absolute Path

This uses the full URL of the image.

Example:

```
<imgsrc="https://example.com/image.jpg">
```

#### 2. Relative Path

This uses the location of the image within the project folder

Example:

```
<imgsrc="images/photo.jpg">
```

## Favicon

Favicon is a small but important element in web design.

When we open a website in a browser, we often see a small icon near the title of the page in the browser tab. This small icon is known as a favicon.

### ▶ Definition

A favicon (short for "favorite icon") can be defined as a small icon associated with a web page, which appears in the browser tab, bookmarks and address bar.

It represents the identity of the website.

### ▶ Purpose of Favicon

1. It helps in branding and recognition of a website.
2. When multiple tabs are open, users can quickly identify a website using its favicon.
3. It also improves the professional appearance of the website.

It is included in the <head> section of the HTML document using the <link> tag.

### ▶ Example

```
<!DOCTYPE html>
<html>
<head>
<title>My Website</title>
<link rel="icon" href="favicon.ico">
</head>
<body>
<h1>Welcome</h1>
</body>
</html>
```

### ▶ Working of Favicon

1. When the browser loads a web page, it checks the <link> tag in the head section.
2. If a favicon is specified, the browser loads that image and displays it in the tab.
3. The favicon is displayed along with the page title.

## HTML Lists

Lists in HTML are used to display data in an organized manner.

### ▶ Definition

An HTML list can be defined as a collection of related items displayed in an ordered or unordered format. Lists are used to group similar elements together.

### ▶ Types of Lists

#### 1. Ordered List

An ordered list is used when the sequence of items is important. The items are displayed in order with numbers (1...) or letters (a-z, A-Z) or Roman numbers (I,II..).

It is created using the <ol> tag, and each item is defined using the <li> tag.

By default, the order list takes the number format.

Example:

```
<ol>
<li>Apple</li>
<li>Samsung</li>
</ol>
```

Ordered lists show items in a sequence.

#### 2. Unordered List

An unordered list is used when the sequence of items is not important. The items are displayed with bullets (disc, square, circle, none).

It is created using the <ul> tag.

Example:

```
<ul>
<li>Java</li>
<li>Python</li>
</ul>
```

Unordered lists show items without sequence.

### 3. Nested List

List in another list is called as nested list in the nested list nested items by default it takes the style type circle and main (unordered) list will take disc bullets.

Example:

```
<ul>
<li>maths</li>
<li>statistics
<ul><li>mean</li>
<li>median</li>
<li>mode</li></ul></li>
</ul>
```

### 4. Description List

A description list is used to define terms and their descriptions. It is created using <dl> tag, <dt> tag is used to specify the data item and <dd> tag Is used to specify the data description of the item.

Example:

```
<dl>
<dt>HTML</dt>
<dd>Markup Language</dd>
</dl>
```

### ▶ Working of Lists

When the browser reads list tags, it automatically arranges the items either in numbered or bulleted format depending on the type of list used.

### ▶ Example

```
<!DOCTYPE html>
<html>
<body>
<h3>ordered list</h3>
<ol>
<li>Apple</li>
<li>Samsung</li>
</ol>
<h3>unordered lists</h3>
```

```
<ul>
<li>Java</li>
<li>Python</li>
</ul>
<h3>description list</h3>
<dl>
<dt>HTML</dt>
<dd>Markup Language</dd>
</dl>
</body>
</html>
```

Output:

# Module: II

# HTML Tables, Creating Forms, HTML Audio

## 2.1 HTML Tables

Tables in HTML are used to display data in a structured and organized format.

In many real-world applications, data is presented in rows and columns, such as marks tables, employee records and product details.

HTML provides table elements to represent such data clearly.

Tables help in organizing data in a tabular form.

▶ **Definition**

An HTML table can be defined as a structure used to arrange data into rows and columns using specific tags.

▶ **Basic Structure of Table**

A table is created using the <table> tag, and it consists of rows and columns.

When creating table, we use style tag <style>.

▶ **Syntax of <style> tag creation or the declaration:**

```
<style>
Table, th, td {
border: 1px solid black;
}
</style>
```

▶ **To represent the width of the table then the syntax is**

```
<table style= "width: 100%">
```

The main tags used are:

1. <table>: defines the table and it is a container for the entire table
2. <tr>: to create table row.

3. <th>: to display the header of the table
4. <td>:Used to display data description order the data

By default, the text in <th> tag elements are bold and centered.

▶ **Example**

```
<!DOCTYPE html>
<html>
<style>
table, th, td {
 border: 1px solid black;
border-collapse: collapse;
}
</style>
<body>
<h2>A Basic HTML Table</h2>
<table style="width:100%">
<tr>
<th>Name</th>
<th>Marks</th>
</tr>
<tr>
<td>John</td>
<td>85</td>
</tr>
<tr>
<td>Mary</td>
<td>90</td>
</tr>
</table>
</body>
</html>
```

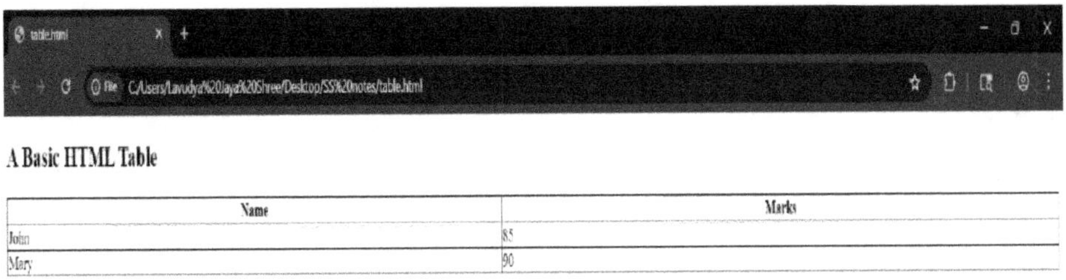
A Basic HTML Table

| Name | Marks |
|---|---|
| John | 85 |
| Mary | 90 |

### ▶ Attributes of Table

**1. Border**: adds different border style for the table

There are different borders such as

a) Dotted (....)

b) Dashed (---)

c) Solid (_)

d) Double (=)

e) Groove

f) Inset

g) Outset

h) Hidden

i) None

j) Ridge

Syntax:

```
<style>
table, th, td {
border-style: dotted;
}
</style>
```

Syntax for table with rounded border (corner):

```
<style>
table, th, td {
  border: 1px solid black;
  border-radius: 10px;
}
table {
  border-collapse: separate;
```

```
 border-spacing: 0;
}
</style>
```

**2. cellpadding**: defines the space between the cell content and its border.

Syntax:

```
<style>
table, th, td {
padding-top: 10px;
padding-bottom: 20px;
padding-left: 15px;
padding-right:30px;
border: 1px solid;
}
</style>
```

**3. cellspacing**: adds space between cells

Syntax:

```
<style>
table {
 border-spacing: 10px;
}
table, th, td {
 border: 1px solid black;
}
</style>
```

## 2.2 Creating Forms in HTML

Forms in HTMLare used to collect information from users. In many websites and web applications, users are required to enter data such as name, password, email or feedback.

This interaction between the user and the website is achieved using forms.

### ▶ Definition

An HTML form can be defined as a container used to collect input from users through different form elements such as text boxes, radio buttons, text field, and submit buttons.Forms are created using the <form> tag.Forms are mainly used for user authentication, registration, searching and feedback collection.

For example:

- Login form
- Registration form
- Contact form

## ▶ Structure of Form

A form contains different input elements enclosed inside the <form> tag.

The main components are:

- Text fields
- Password fields
- Radio buttons
- Checkboxes
- Submit button

## ▶ Important Form Elements

**1. Text Field:** It is used to accept normal text input from the user.

Example:

```
<input type="text">
```

**2. Password Field:** It is used to accept passwords where the entered characters are hidden.

Example:

```
<input type="password">
```

**3. Radio Button:** It is used to select one option from multiple choices.

Example:

```
<input type="radio">
```

**4. Checkbox:** It is used to select multiple options.

Example:

```
<input type="checkbox">
```

**5. Submit Button:** It is used to send form data to the server.

Example:

```
<input type="submit">
```

**Example:**

```
<!DOCTYPE html>
<html>
<head><title>Registration Form</title></head>
```

```
<body>
<h2>Registration Form</h2>
<form>
<label>Full Name:</label><br>
<input type="text" placeholder="Enter your name"><br><br>
<label>Email:</label><br>
<input type="email" placeholder="Enter your email"><br><br>
<label>Password:</label><br>
<input type="password" placeholder="Enter password"><br><br>
<label>Gender:</label><br>
<input type="radio" name="gender"> Male
<input type="radio" name="gender"> Female<br><br>
<label>Course:</label><br>
<input type="checkbox"> CSE
<input type="checkbox"> AIML
<input type="checkbox"> DS<br><br>
<label>Date of Birth:</label><br>
<input type="date"><br><br>
<label>Address:</label><br>
<textarea rows="4" cols="30"></textarea><br><br>
<input type="submit" value="Register">
<input type="reset" value="Clear">
</form></body></html>
```

Output:

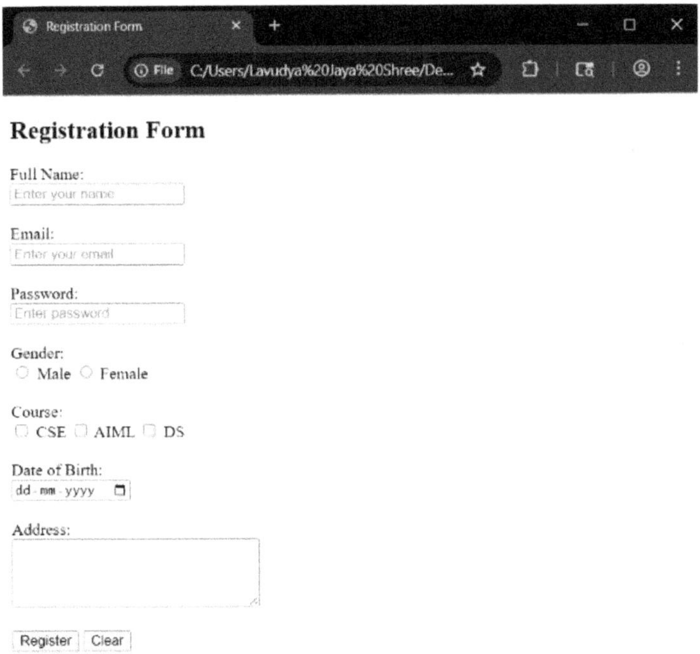


## Attributes of Form

a) **Action**: it specifies where form data should be sent

b) **Method**: it specifies how data is sent (GET or POST)

## 2.3 HTML Audio

Audio in HTML is used to include sound files in web pages.

Multimedia content such as music, voice recordings and sound effects is commonly used to improve user interaction and experience.

For example:

a) Educational websites use recorded lectures

b) Entertainment websites use music and sound effects

### ▶ Definition

HTML audio can be defined as a feature provided by HTML5 that allows inserting and playing audio files directly in a web page using the <audio> tag.

Audio content can be included without external software.

### ▶ Structure of Audio Tag

The audio element contains attributes and source information that specify the audio file.

Example:

```
<audio controls>
<source src="song.mp3" type="audio/mpeg">
</audio>
```

The browser uses the source file to play audio.

**Attributes of Audio Tag:** attributes control the behavior of audio playback.

**1. controls:** it displays audio controls such as play, pause and volume.

**2. autoplay:** It automatically starts playing the audio when the page loads.

**3. loop:** It repeats the audio continuously.

**4. muted:** It starts audio in muted mode.

**Example:**

```
<!DOCTYPE html>
<html>
<body>
<h2>Audio Example</h2>
<audio controls>
<source src="music.mp3" type="audio/mpeg">
</audio>
</body>
</html>
```

## 2.4 HTML Media, Styling Forms, Placeholder

### HTML Media

HTML5 introduced built-in support for multimedia, making it possible to include audio and video directly in web pages without using external plugins.

#### ▶ Definition

HTML media can be defined as multimedia content such as audio and video embedded into web pages using HTML5 tags.Media elements help in delivering rich and interactive content.

#### ▶ Types of Media in HTML

**1. Audio**

Audio is used to include sound content such as music, podcasts and voice recordings. It is implemented using the <audio> tag.

Audio provides sound-based interaction.

### 2. Video

Video is used to display moving visual content such as tutorials, movies and lectures. It is implemented using the <video> tag.

Video provides visual and multimedia communication.

- **HTML Video Tag**

The <video> tag is used to embed videos into a web page. It supports controls such as play, pause and fullscreen mode.

- **Attributes of Video Tag**

  a) **Controls**: it displays video controls

  b) **Autoplay**: It starts video automatically

  c) **Loop**: it repeats the video

  d) **Muted**: It starts video in muted mode

- **Example**

```
<!DOCTYPE html>
<html>
<body>
<video width="400" controls>
<source src="movie.mp4" type="video/mp4">
</video>
</body>
</html>
```

- **Advantages of HTML Media**

It eliminates the need for external plugins.

It improves browser compatibility.

It supports interactive multimedia applications.

HTML5 simplifies multimedia integration.

## Styling Forms

Forms are used to collect user information, but if they are displayed without proper styling, they may look plain and difficult to use.

Therefore, CSS (Cascading Style Sheets) is used to improve the appearance and usability of forms.

Styling forms improves both design and user experience.

### ▶ Definition

Styling forms can be defined as the process of applying CSS properties to form elements in order to improve their appearance, layout and usability.CSS helps in customizing the look of forms.

### ▶ CSS Properties Used in Form Styling

**1. Width and Height:** These properties are used to define the size of input fields.

Example:

```
input {
  width: 200px;
  height: 30px;
}
```

**2. Padding**: Padding adds space inside the input field. It improves readability.

**3. Margin**: Margin adds space outside the elements and helps in proper alignment. Forms look more organized.

**4. Border:** Border is used to define the boundary of form elements.It improves visibility.

**5. Background Color:** This property changes the background color of form elements.Forms become visually attractive.

### ▶ Example (for understanding purpose):

```
<!DOCTYPE html>
<html>
<head>
<style>
    body {
      font-family: Arial;
      background-color: #f2f2f2;}
    form {
  background-color: white;
      width: 350px;
      padding: 20px;
      margin: 50px auto;
      border-radius: 10px;
      box-shadow: 0px 0px 10px gray; }
    h2 {
```

```
        text-align: center;
color: darkblue; }
      input, select, textarea {
        width: 100%;
        padding: 8px;
        margin-top: 5px;
        margin-bottom: 15px;
        border-radius: 5px;
        border: 1px solid gray; }
      input[type="radio"],
      input[type="checkbox"] {
        width: auto;}
      input[type="submit"],
      input[type="reset"] {
        background-color: darkblue;
color: white;
        border: none;
        cursor: pointer; }
      input[type="submit"]:hover,
      input[type="reset"]:hover {
        background-color: navy; }
</style>
</head>
<body>
<h2>Registration Form</h2>
<form>
<label>Full Name:</label><br>
<input type="text" placeholder="Enter your name">
<label>Email:</label><br>
<input type="email" placeholder="Enter your email">
<label>Password:</label><br>
<input type="password" placeholder="Enter password">
<label>Gender:</label><br>
```

```
<input type="radio" name="gender"> Male
<input type="radio" name="gender"> Female<br><br>
<label>Date of Birth:</label><br>
<input type="date">
<input type="submit" value="Register">
<input type="reset" value="Clear">
</form>
</body>
</html>
```

Output:

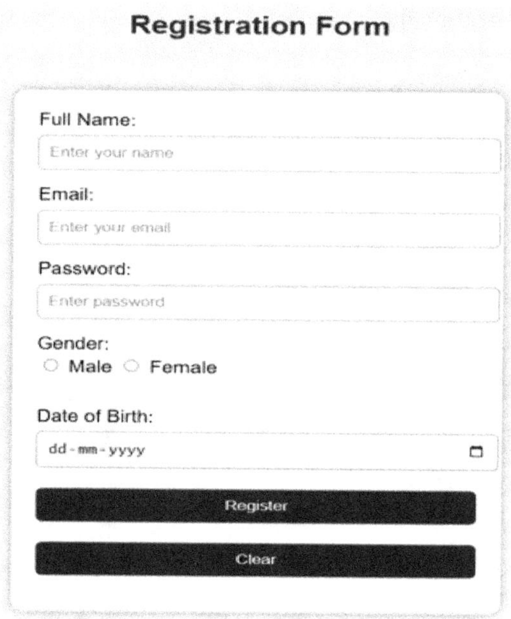


### ▶ Advantages of Styling Forms

1. They improve readability, enhance user interaction and make the interface visually appealing.
2. They also help in creating responsive and professional web pages.
3. Styling improves both functionality and appearance.

## Placeholder in HTML

Placeholder in HTML is used in form input fields to provide guidance to users. It displays temporary text inside the input field as a hint to the user.

Placeholders provide instructions or examples inside form fields before the user enters data.

For example:

a) "Enter your name"

b) "Enter email address"

### ▶ Definition

A placeholder can be defined as a temporary hint or sample text displayed inside an input field to guide the user about the expected input.

It is implemented using the placeholder attribute in HTML.

### ▶ Example

```
<!DOCTYPE html>
<html>
<body>
<form>
  Name:
<input type="text" placeholder="Enter your name"><br><br>
  Email:
<input type="email" placeholder="Enter your email">
</form>
</body>
</html>
```

Output:

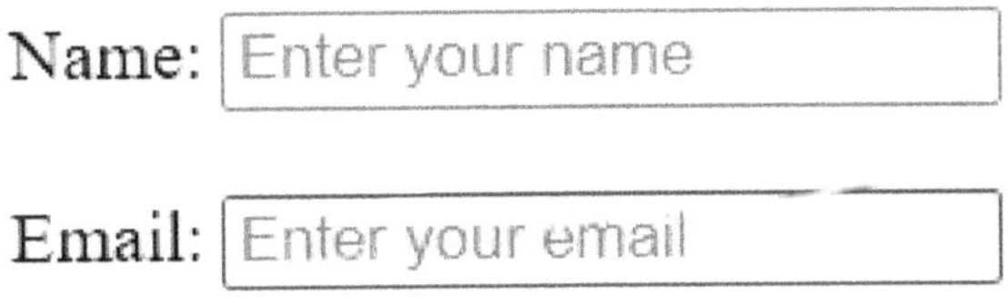


### ▶ Advantages of Placeholder

1. They guide the user, improve readability.
2. They make forms easier to understand.
3. They also reduce the need for additional instructions.

### ▶ Importance of Placeholder

1. It improves the usability of forms and helps users provide correct input.
2. It also makes forms cleaner and more interactive.

## 2.5 Inline and Block Elements, Id vs Class Elements

### Inline and Block Elements

While designing web pages, different HTML elements behave differently in terms of layout and positioning. Some elements occupy the full width of the page, while others occupy only the required space. Based on this behavior, HTML elements are classified into block elements and inline elements.

### Block Elements

▶ **Definition**

A block element can be defined as a HTML element that always starts on a new line and occupies the full available width of the page. Block elements create separate sections in a web page. Block element structure the layout of a page. When the browser encounters a block element, it places it on a separate line.

▶ **Characteristics of Block Elements**

1. They always begin on a new line
2. They occupy full width available
3. Height and width can be adjusted
4. Other elements appear below them

▶ **Examples:**

Some common examples are:

1. <div>
2. <p>
3. <h1> to <h6>
4. <table>

These elements are used for larger sections of content.

### Inline Elements

▶ **Definition**

An inline element can be defined as an HTML element that does not start on a new line and occupies only the required width. Inline elements appear within the same line. Inline elements are used inside block elements.

Inline elements, however, continue within the same line along with surrounding content.

▶ **Characteristics of Inline Elements**

1. They do not start on a new line and occupy only required space
2. Width and height cannot be adjusted easily

3. Multiple inline elements can appear in the same line
4. Inline elements are mainly used for smaller content.

### ▶ Examples of Inline Elements

Some common examples are:

1. <span>
2. <a>
3. <b>
4. <i>

### ▶ Difference Between Inline and Block Elements

| Aspect | Block Element | Inline Element |
|---|---|---|
| Line Behavior | Starts on a new line | Does not start on new line |
| Width | Occupies full width | Occupies only required width |
| Layout | Creates separate section | Appears within same line |
| Examples | <div>, <p> | <span>, <a> |

### ▶ Example

```
<!DOCTYPE html>
<html>
<body>
<p>This is a block element</p>
<span>This is inline element</span>
<span>Another inline element</span>
</body>
</html>
```

### ▶ Importance of Inline and Block Elements

1. These elements are important because they help in controlling the structure and presentation of web pages.
2. Understanding their behavior is essential for proper layout design.

## 2.6 Id vs Class Elements

Id and class attributes in HTML are widely used for identifying and styling elements in web pages.

HTML provides two important attributes called id and class. Although both are used for identification, they differ in their usage and behavior.

When CSS or Java Script accesses an element using id, it selects only that specific element.

When accessed using class, all elements belonging to that class are affected.

Idprovides uniqueness, while class provides grouping.

## Id Attribute

### ▶ Definition

An id attribute can be defined as a unique identifier assigned to a single HTML element. An id is used to uniquely identify a particular element in the web page.

### ▶ Characteristics of Id

1. An id must be unique within the page
2. Only one element can have a particular id
3. It is mainly used for specific styling or JavaScript access
4. Id is used for unique identification.

### ▶ Example of Id

<p id="para1">This is a paragraph.</p>

Here, para1 uniquely identifies the paragraph element.

## Class Attribute

### ▶ Definition

A class attribute can be defined as a name assigned to one or more HTML elements for grouping and styling purposes. Class is used for applying common styles to multiple elements.

### ▶ Characteristics of Class

1. Multiple elements can have the same class name
2. A single element can also have multiple classes
3. It is mainly used for grouping elements with similar styles
4. Class supports reusability.

### ▶ Example of Class

<p class="text">Paragraph One</p>

<p class="text">Paragraph Two</p>

Here, both paragraphs belong to the same class called text.

## ▶ Difference Between Id and Class

| Aspect | Id | Class |
|---|---|---|
| Meaning | Unique identifier | Group identifier |
| Usage | Used for one element | Used for multiple elements |
| Reusability | Cannot be reused | Can be reused |
| CSS Symbol | # symbol | . symbol |
| Purpose | Unique styling or scripting | Common styling |

## ▶ Example

```
<!DOCTYPE html>
<html>
<head>
<style>
#heading {
color: blue;
}
.text {
color: red;
}
</style>
</head>
<body>
<h1 id="heading">Welcome</h1>
<p class="text">Paragraph One</p>
<p class="text">Paragraph Two</p>
</body>
</html>
```

## ▶ Importance of Id and Class

1. Id and class are important because they help in styling and controlling web page elements efficiently.
2. They also improve maintainability and reusability of code.
3. They are essential concepts in HTML and CSS.

# Module: III

## 3.1 CSS3 Basics

Cascading Style Sheets (CSS) is used to format the layout of a web page. These are used the style of HTML.

With CSS you can control the color, font, the size of the text, the spacing between elements, how elements are positioned and laid out, what background images or background colors are to be used, different displays for different devices and screen size and much more.

The word cascading means that a style applied to a parent element will also apply to all children elements within the parent.

The latest version of CSS is CSS3, which provides advanced styling features and better design capabilities.

CSS3 was introduced to separate the design part from the content structure.

CSS3 is important because it improves the appearance, usability and responsiveness of web pages.

### Benefits of CSS3

#### 1. Improved Design and Appearance

CSS3 allows developers to create attractive web pages using colors, gradients, shadows and animations. Websites become visually appealing.

#### 2. Separation of Content and Design

CSS3 separates styling from HTML structure. This makes the code cleaner and easier to manage. Maintenance becomes simple.

#### 3. Reusability

A single CSS file can be applied to multiple web pages. Developers can reuse styles and reduce code duplication.

#### 4. Faster Page Loading

Using external CSS files reduces repeated code in HTML pages. This decreases file size and improves loading speed.CSS3 enhances performance.

#### 5. Responsive Design

CSS3 supports responsive web design using media queries. Websites can automatically adjust to different screen sizes such as mobiles, tablets and desktops.CSS3 improves compatibility across devices.

### 6. Animation and Effects

CSS3 provides features such as transitions, transformations and animations without requiring JavaScript. Websites become more interactive.

### 7. Easy Maintenance

Changes made in a CSS file are automatically reflected in all connected web pages. Updating design becomes easier.

## CSS3 Syntax

CSS3 syntax defines the structure used for writing CSS rules. CSS is used to apply styles to HTML elements, and these styles are written using a specific format called syntax.

### ▶ Definition

CSS3 syntax can be defined as the standard structure used to write style rules for HTML elements. A CSS rule specifies which element should be styled and what style should be applied.

### ▶ Structure of CSS Syntax

A CSS rule mainly consists of two parts:

1. Selector
2. Declaration Block

The selector finds the HTML element to be styled, and the declaration block contains the styling properties and values.

CSS syntax defines both the target element and its style.

Basic Structure of CSS Syntax:

```
Selector {
  Property : Value;
}
```

**1. Selector:** The selector specifies the HTML element on which the style should be applied.

Example:

'p' selects all paragraph elements.

**2. Property:** The property defines what aspect of the element should be styled.

Examples:

a) color
b) font-size
c) background-color

**3. Value:** The value specifies how the property should appear.

Example:

```
color: red;
```

Here, red is the value assigned to the color property.

**4. Declaration Block:** The declaration block is enclosed within curly braces { } and contains one or more property-value pairs separated by semicolons.

### ▶ Example

```
<!DOCTYPE html>
<html>
<head>
<style>
p {
color: blue;
  font-size: 20px;
}
</style>
</head>
<body>
<p>This is a paragraph.</p>
</body>
</html>
```

Output

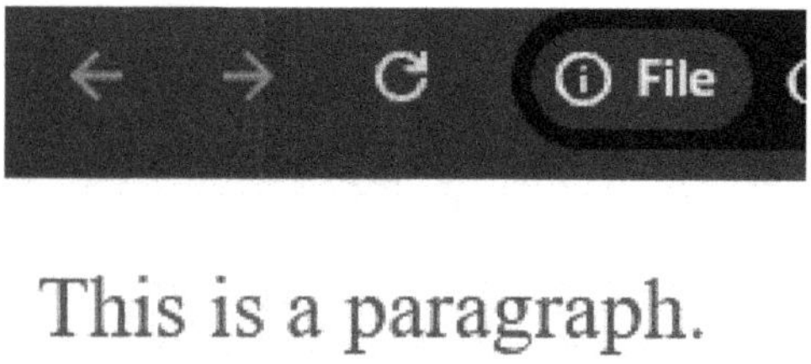


For example, a developer may use CSS syntax to change the text color of headings or adjust the size of buttons.

Thus, CSS syntax is used in every styled web page.

## 3.2 CSS Comments

Comments in CSS are used to add explanationof the code part inside CSS code.

While developing web pages, developers often write large amounts of CSS code. In such situations, comments help in improving readability and understanding of the code.

Comments are ignored by the browser and are meant only for developers.

Comments help developers explain the purpose of styles, separate sections of code and make the stylesheet easier to understand.

### ▶ Definition

A CSS comment can be defined as a note or explanatory text written inside CSS code that is not executed or displayed by the browser.

### ▶ Syntax of CSS Comments

A comment begins with /* and ends with */.

Anything written between these symbols is treated as a comment and ignored by the browser.

### ▶ Example

```
<!DOCTYPE html>
<html>
<head>
<style>
/* Styling for paragraph */
p {
color: blue;
   font-size: 20px;
}
</style>
</head>
<body>
<p>This is a paragraph.</p>
</body>
</html>
```

### Advantages of CSS Comments

1. They improve readability.
2. They help in debugging and make code easier to maintain.

3. They also help developers understand different sections of the stylesheet.
4. Comments improve code management.
5. CSS comments are important because they improve understanding and maintenance of stylesheets.

## 3.3 Including CSS3 in HTML Documents

CSS is used to style and design web pages, but in order to apply styles, CSS rules must first be connected to the HTML document.

HTML provides different methods for including CSS. Each method has its own purpose and usage depending on the requirement of the webpage.

**Methods of Including CSS:** The three main methods are:

1. Inline CSS
2. Internal CSS
3. External CSS

CSS can be added directly, internally or externally.

### 1. Inline CSS

It uses the style attribute of an HTML element.

Inline CSS is a method of applying styling directly to individual HTML elements by using the "style" attribute within the HTML tag,allowing for specific styling of individual elements within the HTML document, overriding any external or internal styles.

Inline CSS has the highest priority. Any styles that are defined in the internal and external sheets are overridden by inline sheets

```
<h1 style="color:blue;">A Blue Heading</h1>
```

### 2. Internal or Embedded CSS

It is defined within the HTML document's <style>element.It applies styles to specified HTML elements.The CSS rules set should be within HTML file in the head section i.e., the CSS is embedded within the <style> tag inside the head section of the HTML file.Internal stands second in the priority list and overrides the styles in the external style sheet.

Example:

```
<style>
.main {
text-align:center;
}
.h {
```

```
color: #009900;
font-size: 50px;
font-weight: bold;
}
.p {
font-style: bold;
font-size: 20px;
}
</style>
```

(OR)

```
body {
background-color: lightblue;
}
h1 {
color: white;
text-align: center;
}
p{
font-size:20px;
font-family:verdana;
}
```

## 3. External CSS

It contains separate CSS files that contain only style properties with the help of tag attributes (For example class, id, heading, ... etc).

CSS property is written in a separate file with a .css extension and should be linked to the HTML document using a link tag.

It means that, for each element, style can be set only once and will be applied across web pages.

External style sheets have the least priority. If there are no styles defined either in inline or internal style sheet then external style sheet rules are applied for the HTML tags.

HTML Input:

```
<link rel="stylesheet" href="style.css">
```

Style.css file

```
body {
background-color: powderblue;
}
.main {
 text-align: center;
 }
 .p {
color: #009900;
font-size: 50px;
font-weight: bold;
}
#h {
 font-style: bold;
font-size: 20px;
```

## 3.4 CSS3-Selectors

CSS selectors are used to "find" (or select) the HTML elements you want to style.

### Element Type Selector

The element selector selects HTML elements based on the element name.

- **Syntax**

```
p {
text-align: center;
color: red;
}
```

### Id Selector

The id selector uses the id attribute of an HTML element to select a specific element.The id of an element is unique within a page, so the id selector is used to select one unique element.

To select an element with a specific id, write a hash (#) character, followed by the id of the element.

**Syntax**

```
#p1 {
text-align: center;
color: red; }
```

## Class Selector

The class selector selects HTML elements with a specific class attribute.

To select elements with a specific class, write a period (.) character, followed by the class name.

▶ **Syntax**

```
.center {
text-align: center;
color: red;
}
```

## Universal Selector

The universal selector (*) selects all HTML elements on the page.

▶ **Syntax**

```
* {
text-align: center;
color: yellow;
}
```

## Grouping Selector

The grouping selector selects all the HTML elements with the same style definitions.

▶ **Syntax**

```
h1 {
text-align: center;
color: red;
}
```

# 3.5 CSS-Styles

CSS3 styles are used to improve the appearance and presentation of web pages.

Using CSS3 styles, developers can change colors, backgrounds, fonts, text appearance, links, lists and table design.

These styles help in creating attractive, readable and user-friendly websites.

## CSS Color

Colors are used to improve the visual appearance of web pages. They can be applied to text, backgrounds, borders and other elements.Colors help in making web pages attractive and readable.

CSS3 supports different methods for defining colors.

**1. Color Name**

```
p {
color: red;
}
```

**2. RGB Value (Red, Green, Blue)**

```
p {
color: rgb(0,0,255);
}
```

**3. Hexadecimal Value**

Each color in HTML has unique hexadecimal value.

```
p {
color: #00FF00;
}
```

## CSS Background

Background properties are used to control the appearance of the background of an element or webpage. Background styling improves the visual design of the page.

### ▶ Background Properties

**1. Background Color**

```
body {
  background-color: lightblue;
}
```

**2. Background Image**

```
body {
  background-image: url("image.jpg");
}
```

**3. Background Repeat**

Controls repetition of background image.

```
body {
  background-repeat: no-repeat;
}
```

#### 4. Background Position

Defines image position.

```
body {
  background-position: center;
}
```

## CSS Fonts

Fonts define the style and appearance of text.

### Font Properties

**1. Font Family:** it defines the type of font.

```
p {
  font-family: Arial;
}
```

**2. Font Size:** it defines text size.

```
p {
  font-size: 20px;
}
```

**3. Font Weight:** it defines thickness of text.

```
p {
  font-weight: bold;
}
```

**4. Font Style:** it defines italic style.

```
p {
  font-style: italic;
}
```

## CSS Text

Text properties are used to control alignment, spacing and decoration of text.

### ▶ Text Properties

#### 1. Text Color

```
p {
color: blue;
}
```

**2. Text Alignment**

```
h1 {
  text-align: center;
}
```

**3. Text Decoration**

```
a {
  text-decoration: none;
}
```

**4. Text Transform**

```
p {
  text-transform: uppercase;
}
```

## CSS Links

Links can be styled using colors, hover effects and decorations. Styled links improve navigation and interaction.

▶ **Link States**

**1. Normal Link**

```
a {
color: blue;
}
```

**2. Hover Effect**

```
a:hover {
color: red;
}
```

**3. Visited Link**

```
a:visited {
color: green;
}
```

## CSS Lists

CSS can modify list bullets, numbering and spacing.List styling improves presentation.

▶ **List Properties**

**1. List Style Type**

```
ul {
  list-style-type: square;
}
```

**2. List Style Position**

```
ul {
  list-style-position: inside;
}
```

## CSS Tables

CSS improves table appearance using borders, spacing and colors. Styled tables become easier to read.

### ▶ Table Properties

**1. Border**

```
table, th, td {
  border: 1px solid black;
}
```

**2. Padding**

```
td {
  padding: 10px;
}
```

**3. Border Collapse**

```
table {
  border-collapse: collapse;
}
```

# Module: IV

## 4.1 CSS3 – Box Model

Every HTML element in CSS is treated as a rectangular box. This box consists of:

- Content
- Padding
- Border
- Margin

The box model defines the structure and spacing of elements.

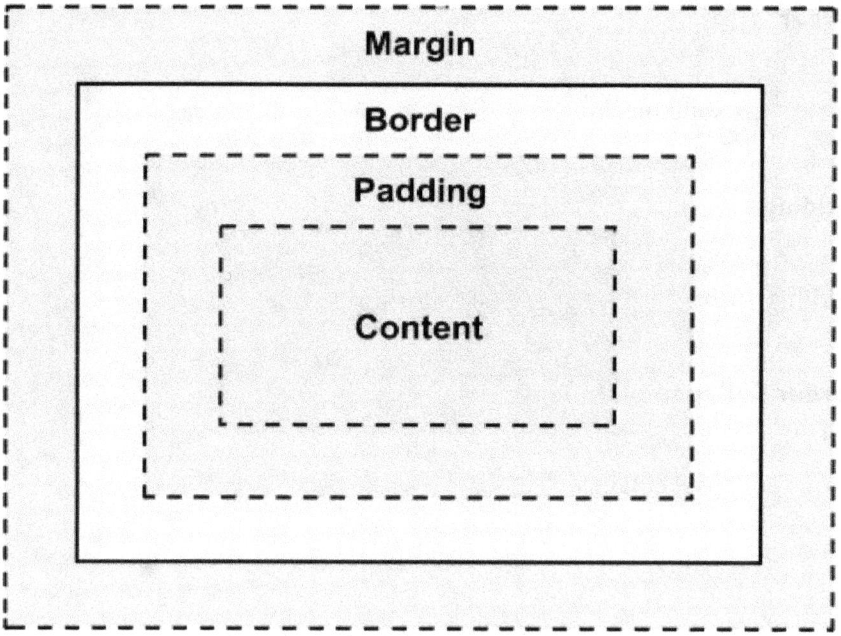


**Fig 4.1: CSS3 Box Model**

### Margin

While designing web pages, it is important to maintain proper spacing between elements so that the content looks clean, organized and readable.

CSS3 provides the margin property to create space outside an element.

Margin helps in separating one element from another and improves the overall layout of the webpage.

When margin is applied to an element, the browser creates transparent space outside the border of that element. This space separates the element from nearby elements.

### ▶ Definition of Margin

Margin can be defined as the transparent space outside the border of an HTML element. It creates distance between one element and another element. Margin controls external spacing in web pages.

### ▶ Need for Margin

If multiple elements are placed very close to each other, the webpage may look crowded and difficult to read.

Margin creates proper spacing and improves visual presentation.

Margin improves readability and webpage organization.

### ▶ Types of Margin Properties

CSS provides different margin properties to control spacing on different sides of an element.

**1. margin-top:** it is used to add space above the element.

```
p{
  margin-top: 20px;
}
```

**2. margin-right:** it is used to add space on the right side.

```
p{
  margin-right: 30px;
}
```

**3. margin-bottom:** it is used to add space below the element.

```
p{
  margin-bottom: 20px;
}
```

**4. margin-left:** it is used to add space on the left side.

```
p{
  margin-left: 30px;
}
```

**5. Shorthand Margin Property:** Instead of writing all sides separately, CSS allows shorthand notation (single line syntax) to reduce code length.

```
p{
```

```
  margin: 20px 30px 20px 30px;
}
```

Order can be top, right, bottom and left.

### Advantages of Margin

- It improves readability of the web page.
- It prevents overlapping of elements. For example, a web page has 2 buttons attached together with no spacing, makes user confuse. To prevent this margin is used.
- It creates clean layouts of webpage.
- It improves webpage presentation

## 4.2 Padding

In webpage design, proper spacing inside elements is very important for improving readability and appearance.

CSS provides the padding property. Padding creates space between the content and the border of an element.

When padding is applied to an element, the browser creates space between the content and the border.

### Definition

Padding can be defined as the transparent space between the content of an element and its border. Padding controls internal spacing within an element.

### Types of Padding Properties

CSS provides different padding properties for controlling spacing on different sides.

**1. padding-top:** it adds space above the content.

```
p {
  padding-top: 20px;
}
```

**2. padding-right:** it adds space on the right side of content.

```
p {
  padding-right: 30px;
}
```

**3. padding-bottom:** it adds space below the content.

```
p {
  padding-bottom: 20px;
```

```
}
```

**4. padding-left:** it adds space on the left side of content.

```
p {
  padding-left: 30px;
}
```

**5. Shorthand Padding Property:** CSS allows shorthand notation for writing all padding values together.

```
p {
  padding: 20px 30px 20px 30px;
}
```

Order:

- Top
- Right
- Bottom
- Left

### Advantages of Padding

- It improves readability
- It prevents content from touching borders
- It creates attractive layouts
- It enhances user experience

### Difference Between Padding and Margin

| Aspect | **Padding** | **Margin** |
|---|---|---|
| Position | Inside border | Outside border |
| Purpose | Creates internal spacing | Creates external spacing |
| Background Color | Affected by background | Not affected |

## 4.3 Border

CSS provides the border property. A border is the visible boundary that surrounds the padding and content of an element. It helps in highlighting elements and improving webpage structure.

Borders help in distinguishing elements from one another. They improve visual clarity and make webpage components easier to identify.

For example:

- Borders around buttons
- Borders around tables
- Borders around forms

### ▶ Position of Border in Box Model

The border is placed outside the padding and inside the margin. It acts as a boundary around the content and padding area.

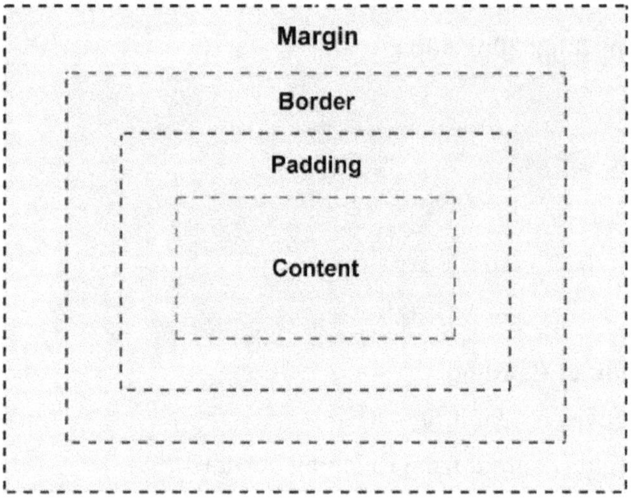


**Fig 4.2: CSS3 Box Model Showing Border**

### ▶ Definition of Border

A border can be defined as the visible line or boundary surrounding the padding and content of an HTML element.

**Border Properties:** CSS provides different properties for controlling borders

**1. border-style**: it defines the style of the border.

Common styles:

- solid
- dotted
- dashed
- double

**Example**

```
p {
  border-style: solid;
```

}

**2. border-width:** it defines thickness of the border.

**Example**

```
p {
  border-width: 3px;
}
```

**3. border-color:** it defines color of the border.

**Example**

```
p {
  border-color: blue;
}
```

**4. Shorthand Border Property:** instead of writing separate properties, all values can be written together.

**Example**

```
p {
  border: 2px solid red;
}
```

Order:

- Width
- Style
- Color

**Different Border Styles**

| Border Style | **Appearance** |
|---|---|
| solid | Continuous line |
| dotted | Dots |
| dashed | Broken line |
| double | Double line |

**Example**

```
<!DOCTYPE html>
<html>
<head>
<style>
p {
```

```
  border: 3px solid blue;
  padding: 10px;
}
</style>
</head>
<body>
<p>This is a bordered paragraph.</p>
</body>
</html>
```

Output

### ▶ Advantages of Border

- It improves visual clarity
- It highlights important elements
- It separates content into sections
- It enhances webpage design

## 4.4 Outline

In webpage design, developers sometimes need to highlight elements without affecting the actual layout of the page. For this purpose, CSS provides the outline property.

An outline is similar to a border, but it is drawn outside the border of an element. Unlike borders, outlines do not occupy space in the layout.

Outlines are mainly used for highlighting and focusing elements.

The outline is drawn outside the border area of the element. It does not affect padding, border or margin calculations.

When outline properties are applied, the browser draws a line outside the border of the element. Since it does not take layout space, the size of the element remains unchanged.

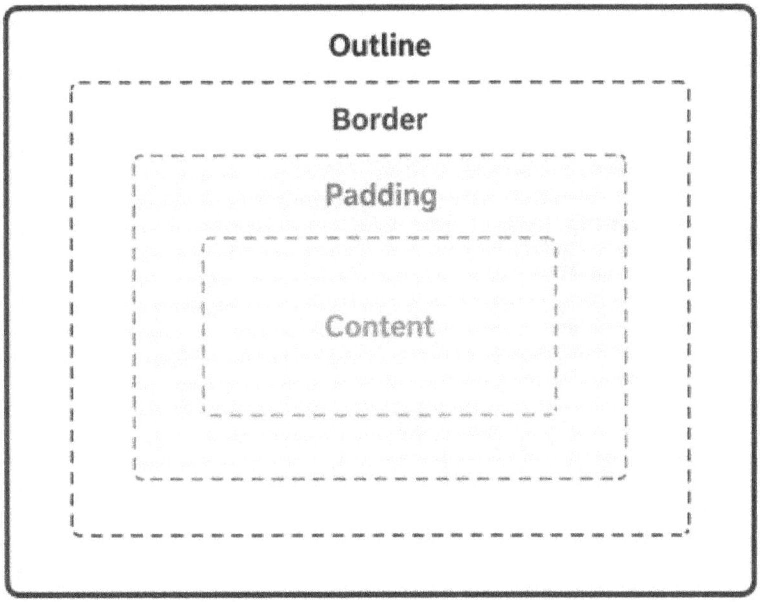


**Fig 4.3: CSS3 Box Model Showing Outline**

▶ **Definition**

An outline can be defined as a line drawn outside the border of an HTML element for highlighting purposes. Outline provides an external visual effect.

**Outline Properties:** CSS provides different properties for controlling outlines.

**1. outline-style:** It defines the style of the outline.

Common styles are solid, dotted, dashed and double

**Example**

```
p {
  outline-style: solid;
}
```

**2. outline-width**: It defines thickness of the outline.

**Example**

```
p {
  outline-width: 3px;
}
```

**3. outline-color**: It defines color of the outline.

**Example**

```
p {
```

```
  outline-color: red;
}
```

**4. Shorthand Outline Property**: All outline properties can be written together.

**Example**

```
p {
  outline: 3px solid blue;
}
```

### ▶ Example

```
<!DOCTYPE html>
<html><head>
<style>
input:focus {
  outline: 3px solid blue;
}
</style></head>
<body><input type="text" placeholder="Enter Name"></body>
</html>
```

Output:

### ▶ Advantages of Outline

- It highlights elements clearly
- It does not affect layout size
- It improves accessibility
- It useful for focus indication

Thus, outlines improve usability and webpage interaction.

### ▶ Difference Between Border and Outline

| **Aspect** | **Border** | **Outline** |
|---|---|---|
| Position | Around padding | Outside border |
| Layout Space | Takes space | Does not take space |
| Purpose | Structural boundary | Highlighting |
| Shape | Follows element shape | External highlight |

## 4.5 Visibility

CSS provides the visibility property. It controls whether an element should be visible or hidden on the webpage.

Examples:

- Hiding menu items
- Displaying messages dynamically
- Showing popups or notifications

- **Definition:** Visibility can be defined as a CSS property used to control whether an HTML element is visible or hidden on a webpage.
- **Visibility Property Values:** CSS provides different values for the visibility property.

### 1. visibility: visible

This is the default value. The element is displayed normally.

**Example**

```
p {
  visibility: visible;
}
```

### 2. visibility: hidden

This hides the element from the webpage, but the space occupied by the element is still reserved.

**Example**

```
p {
  visibility: hidden:}
```

### ▶ Example

```
<!DOCTYPE html>
<html>
<head>
<style>
.hiddenText {
  visibility: hidden;
}
</style>
</head>
```

```
<body>
<p>This paragraph is visible.</p>
<p class="hiddenText">
This paragraph is hidden.
</p>
</body>
</html>
```

Output:

This paragraph is visible.

### ▶ Advantages of Visibility

1. It controls appearance dynamically
2. It maintains webpage layout
3. It is useful for interactive interfaces
4. It supports user-friendly design.

## Display

CSS provides the display property to control how elements are displayed on the webpage. It determines whether an element behaves as a block element, inline element or hidden element.

Different webpage components require different layouts.

**Examples:**

- Navigation menus displayed inline
- Sections displayed as blocks
- Hiding elements completely

Without the display property, proper webpage layout and alignment would not be possible.

### ▶ Definition

The display property can be defined as a CSS property used to specify how an HTML element should be displayed on a webpage.

### ▶ Common Values of Display Property

#### 1. display: block

This value makes the element behave as a block element which starts on a new line and occupies full width available.

**Example**

```
p {
  display: block;
}
```

**2. display: inline**

This value makes the element behave as an inline element. It does not start on a new line and occupies only required width

**Example**

```
span {
  display: inline;
}
```

**3. display: inline-block**

This combines features of both inline and block elements. It appears in the same line where width and height can be adjusted

**Example**

```
div {
  display: inline-block;
}
```

**4. display: none**

This completely hides the element from the webpage. Here, element is not displayed and space is also removed.

**Example**

```
p {
  display: none;
}
```

**Example**

```
<!DOCTYPE html>
<html>
<head>
<style>
.blockElement {
  display: block;
  background-color: lightblue;
```

```
}
.inlineElement {
   display: inline;
   background-color: yellow;
}
</style>
</head>
<body>
<div class="blockElement">Block Element</div>
<span class="inlineElement">Inline Element</span>
<span class="inlineElement">Another Inline Element</span>
</body>
</html>
```

Output:

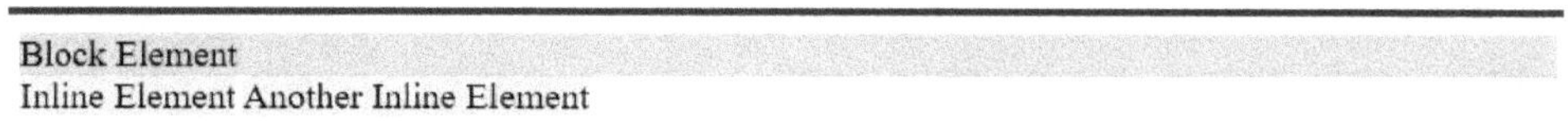


**▶ Advantages of Display Property**

- It controls webpage layout
- It supports responsive design
- It helps in hiding/showing elements
- It improves alignment and positioning

## 4.6 Multiple Columns

CSS3 introduced the multiple column feature, which allows content to be divided into several columns easily.

When large text content is displayed in a single wide paragraph, it may become difficult for users to read comfortably. Multiple columns divide the content into smaller sections and improve readability.

**▶ Definition**

Multiple columns can be defined as a CSS3 feature used to divide content into two or more vertical columns within a webpage element.

**▶ CSS3 Multiple Column Properties**

### 1. column-count

The column-count property specifies the number of columns into which content should be divided.

**Example**

```
div {
  column-count: 3;
}
```

**2. column-gap**

The column-gap property defines the space between columns.

**Example**

```
div {
  column-gap: 30px;
}
```

**3. column-rule**

The column-rule property adds a line between columns.

**Example**

```
div {
  column-rule: 2px solid black;
}
```

**4. column-width**

The column-width property defines the width of each column.

**Example**

```
div {
  column-width: 200px;
}
```

▶ **Example**

```
<!DOCTYPE html>
<html>
<head>
<style>
div {
  column-count: 3;
  column-gap: 20px;
  column-rule: 2px solid gray;
}
```

```
</style>
</head>
<body>
<div>
CSS3 multiple columns allow content to be divided into several vertical sections. This improves readability and presentation of large text content on webpages.
</div>
</body>
</html>
```

CSS3 multiple columns allow content to be divided into several vertical sections. This improves readability and presentation of large text content on webpages.

### ► Advantages

- It improves readability
- It creates attractive layouts
- It organizes large content efficiently
- It provides newspaper-style presentation

## 4.7 Java Script

### Introduction to Java Script

- JavaScript has been created by Eed Sen Elith.
- It is not a fully programming language but a partially programming language.
- It is also called as object-based language.
- HTML code with programming code is called Java script.
- Earlier, it used to be called as Live script.
- In the year 1995, Netscape browser introduced live script.
- In 1996, first version was introduced i.e.,1.0.
- The latest version is 1.8.5 which was introduced in the year 2021.
- Java Script is a client-server application where the client gives the request and server gives the response.
- In JavaScript client server response is very slow compared to the PHP programming.
- JavaScript can be defined as a high-level scripting language used to add interactivity, dynamic behavior and functionality to web pages.

- It works together with HTML and CSS.
- JavaScript enables:
- Form validation
- Dynamic content updates
- Animations
- Interactive menus
- Calculations

### Features of JavaScript

**1. Lightweight Language:** JavaScript is lightweight and executes quickly inside the browser.

**2. Interpreted Language:** JavaScript code is interpreted directly by the browser without separate compilation.Execution becomes faster and easier.

**3. Dynamic Nature:** It allows content to change dynamically without reloading the webpage.

**4. Event-Based Programming:** JavaScript responds to user actions such as clicks, typing and mouse movements.

**5. Cross-Platform Support:** It works in all modern web browsers and operating systems.

6. Javascript is a case sensitive language.

- JavaScript can be included in HTML documents in three ways:
    1. Inline JavaScript
    2. Internal JavaScript
    3. External JavaScript

JavaScript can be embedded directly or linked externally.

### Example:

```
<!DOCTYPE html>
<html>
<body>
<button onclick="showMessage()">
Click Me
</button>
<script>
function showMessage() {
  alert("believe in yourself");
```

```
}
</script>
</body>
</html>
```

Output:

In the above example, a button is created using HTML and when the user clicks the button, JavaScript function is executed and then the alert() function displays a popup message.

### ▶ Applications of JavaScript

JavaScript is widely used in:

- Form validation
- Online calculators
- Interactive menus
- Games
- Web applications
- Animations

### ▶ Advantages of JavaScript

- It improves webpage interactivity and reduces server load.
- It provides immediate user response.
- It supports dynamic content.
- It works on all browsers.

## 4.8 JavaScript and Forms

Forms are used to collect data from users, such as login details, registration information and feedback.

However, if users enter incorrect or incomplete data. To solve this issue, JavaScript is used with forms for validation and interaction.

### ▶ Definition

JavaScript and Forms refer to the use of JavaScript programming to control, validate and process HTML form data dynamically before sending it to the server.

- If form data is submitted without validation:
    - Required fields may remain empty
    - Invalid email formats may be entered
    - Weak passwords may be accepted

JavaScript checks the data before submission and displays immediate feedback to the user.

### ▶ Functions of JavaScript in Forms

**1. Form Validation:** Validation checks whether the entered data is correct. It prevents incorrect data submission.

Examples:Empty field checking, password length checking, and mail format validation

**2. Dynamic Interaction:** JavaScript can dynamically show or hide form fields based on user actions.

Example:Showing additional options after selecting a checkbox

**3. Automatic Calculations**: JavaScript can perform calculations within forms.

Examples: total price calculation, percentage calculation

**4. User Feedback**: JavaScript provides instant messages and alerts to users.

Examples:"Password is too short"

### ▶ Form Validation Process

- Step 1:User enters data into form fields.
- Step 2:JavaScript checks the entered data.
- Step 3:If data is invalid, an error message is displayed.
- Step 4:If data is correct, the form is submitted.

### ▶ Accessing Form Elements in JavaScript

JavaScript accesses form fields using:

- document.forms
- getElementById()
- name attribute

**Example:**

```
<!DOCTYPE html>
<html>
<body>
<form onsubmit="return validateForm()">
```

```
Name:
<input type="text" id="name">
<input type="submit" value="Submit">
</form>
<script>
function validateForm() {
  var x =
document.getElementById("name").value;
  if(x == "") {
    alert("Name must be filled out");
    return false;
  }
 return true;
}
</script>
</body>
</html>
```

Output:

Here, the user enters data into the text box, when submit button is clicked, JavaScript function executes. If the field is empty, an alert message appears. Form submission is stopped until valid data is entered

### ▶ Advantages of JavaScript in Forms

- It reduces invalid submissions and improves user experience
- It provides immediate feedback and reduces server load
- It supports interactive forms

## 4.9 Functions, Operators, Conditional Statements and Loops

### JavaScript Form Variables

A variable acts as a storage container that temporarily holds data during program execution. Form variables help JavaScript access, validate and manipulate user input dynamically.

- **Definition of Variable:** A variable can be defined as a named memory location used to store data temporarily during program execution.

When a user enters data into a form, JavaScript must store that data in variables in order to:

- Validate input
- Perform calculations
- Display messages
- Process form information

Without variables, JavaScript cannot handle user-entered data effectively.

#### Types of Variables in JavaScript

**1. var:** The var keyword is the traditional method used for declaring variables. Data is stored inside the variable name

**Example:** var name = "John";

**2. let:** The let keyword is used for declaring block-level variables.

**Example:** let age = 20;

**3. const:** The const keyword is used for constant values that should not change.

**Example:** const country = "India";

#### Accessing Form Data Using Variables

JavaScript accesses form elements using methods such as:

- getElementById()
- document.forms[]

The entered value is then stored in a variable.

#### Example:

```
<!DOCTYPE html>
<html>
<body>
<form>
Enter Name:
```

```
<input type="text" id="username">
<button type="button"
onclick="showName()">
Submit
</button>
</form>
<script>
function showName() {
var name =
document.getElementById("username").value;
alert("Welcome " + name);
}
</script>
</body>
</html>
```

Output:

Here, user enters a name into the text boxandJavaScript reads the value using getElementById(). The value is stored in the variable name. The alert box displays the entered name.

## ▶ Applications of Form Variables

Form variables are widely used in:

- Login systems
- Registration forms
- Online examinations
- Shopping websites
- Feedback forms

For example, login forms store username and password values in variables before validation.

## JavaScript Functions

### ▶ Definition of Function

A function can be defined as a named block of code that performs a specific task and executes only when it is called.

Without functions, developers would need to repeat the same code multiple times. This would make programs lengthy and difficult to maintain.

Functions help in reducing repeated code, improving readability, simplifying debugging and organizing programs.

### ▶ Structure of a Function

A JavaScript function mainly consists of:

- Function keyword
- Function name
- Parameters (optional)
- Function body

### ▶ Syntax of Function

```
function functionName() {
  // statements
}
```

### ▶ Types of Functions

**1. Function Without Parameters**: This type of function does not accept any input values.

**Example:**

```
function showMessage() {
  alert("Welcome to JavaScript");
}
showMessage();
```

**2. Function With Parameters:** This type of function accepts input values called parameters.

**Example:**

```
function add(a, b) {
  alert(a + b);
}
add(10, 20);
```

**3. Function With Return Value:** A function can also return a value using the return statement.

**Example:**

```
function square(x) {
   return x * x;
}
var result = square(5);
alert(result);
```

**Example**

```
<!DOCTYPE html>
<html>
<body>
<button onclick="greet()">
Click Here
</button>
<script>
function greet() {
   alert("Hello Student");
}
</script>
</body>
</html>
```

Output:

Here, a button is created using HTML. When the button is clicked, the greet() function executes. The alert box displays a message

## JavaScript Operators

In programming; calculations, comparisons and logical decisions are very common tasks. JavaScript provides operators to perform these operations efficiently.

Operators work together with operands to produce a result.

For example:a + b

Here:

- + is the operator
- a and b are operands

## Definition of Operator

An operator can be defined as a special symbol used to perform operations on variables and values.

## Types of JavaScript Operators

JavaScript provides different categories of operators.

- Arithmetic Operators
- Assignment Operators
- Comparison Operators
- Logical Operators
- Increment and Decrement Operators
- Conditional Operator

**1. Arithmetic Operators**: Arithmetic operators are used to perform mathematical calculations.

| Operator | Purpose | Example |
|---|---|---|
| + | Addition | a + b |
| - | Subtraction | a - b |
| * | Multiplication | a * b |
| / | Division | a / b |
| % | Modulus | a % b |

**Example**

```
var a = 10;
var b = 5;
document.write(a + b);
```

**2. Assignment Operators**: Assignment operators are used to assign values to variables.

| **Operator** | **Purpose** |
|---|---|
| = | Assign value |
| += | Add and assign |
| -= | Subtract and assign |

**Example**

var x = 10;

x += 5:

**3. Comparison Operators:** Comparison operators compare two values and return either true or false.

| Operator | Purpose |
|---|---|
| == | Equal to |
| != | Not equal to |
| > | Greater than |
| < | Less than |

**Example**

var a = 10;

document.write(a > 5);

**4. Logical Operators:** Logical operators combine multiple conditions.

| Operator | Purpose |
|---|---|
| && | Logical AND |
| | |
| ! | Logical NOT |

**Example**

var age = 20;

document.write(age > 18 && age < 30);

**5. Increment and Decrement Operators:** These operators increase or decrease variable values.

| Operator | Purpose |
|---|---|
| ++ | Increment |
| -- | Decrement |

**Example**

var x = 5;

x++;

**6. Conditional Operator:** The conditional operator is also called the ternary operator.

**Example**

var age = 20;

var result =

(age >= 18) ? "Adult" : "Minor";

### ▶ Advantages of Operators

Operators provide several advantages:

- Simplify calculations
- Support decision-making
- Improve program efficiency
- Reduce code complexity
- Enable dynamic processing

## 4.10 Java Script Conditional Statements and Loops

### ▶ Conditional Statements

Conditional statements can be defined as statements used to make decisions in a program based on specific conditions.Without conditional statements, programs cannot make decisions dynamically.

### ▶ Types of Conditional Statements

JavaScript provides different types of conditional statements.

- if statement
- if...else statement
- else if ladder
- switch statement

**1. if Statement:** The if statement executes code only when the condition is true.

**Syntax:**

```
if(condition) {
  // statements
}
```

**Example**

```
var age = 20;
if(age >= 18) {
  alert("Eligible to Vote");
}
```

**2. if...else Statement:** The if...else statement provides two possible execution paths.

**Syntax:**

```
if(condition) {
  // true statements
```

```
}
else {
  // false statements
}
```

**Example**

```
var marks = 40;
if(marks >= 35) {
  alert("Pass");
}
else {
  alert("Fail");
}
```

**3. else if Ladder**: The else if ladder is used when multiple conditions need to be checked.

**Example**

```
var marks = 85;
if(marks >= 90) {
  alert("Grade A");
}
else if(marks >= 75) {
  alert("Grade B");
}
else {
alert("Grade C");
}
```

**4. switch Statement:** The switch statement is used when many conditions depend on one variable.

**Example**

```
var day = 2;
switch(day) {
case 1:
  alert("Monday");
  break;
```

```
case 2:
  alert("Tuesday");
  break;
default:
  alert("Invalid Day");
}
```

## Loops in JavaScript

A loop can be defined as a control structure used to repeatedly execute a block of code until a specified condition becomes false.

**Examples:**

- Displaying numbers
- Processing arrays
- Repeating calculations

### ▶ Types of Loops

JavaScript provides different types of loops.

- for loop
- while loop
- do...while loop

**1. for Loop**: The for loop is commonly used when the number of repetitions is known.

**Syntax**

```
for(initialization;
condition;
increment) {
  // statements
}
```

**Example:**

```
for(var i = 1; i <= 5; i++) {
  document.write(i);
}
```

**2. while Loop:** The while loop executes as long as the condition remains true.

**Example:**

```
var i = 1;
while(i<= 5) {
document.write(i);
i++;
}
```

**3. do...while Loop:** The do...while loop executes at least once even if the condition is false.

**Example**

```
var i = 1;
do {
document.write(i);
i++;
} while(i<= 5);
```

## ▶ Advantages of Conditional Statements and Loops

They provide several advantages:

- Support decision-making
- Reduce repeated coding
- Improve program efficiency
- Simplify complex tasks
- Enable automation

They improve programming flexibility and control.

# Module: V

## 5.1 Arrays

### ▶ JavaScript Arrays

In programming, there are situations where many related values must be stored and processed together.

For example:

- List of student names
- Marks of subjects
- Product prices
- Employee records

If separate variables are used for each value, the program becomes lengthy and difficult to manage.

### ▶ Definition of Array

An array can be defined as a collection of multiple values stored under a single variable name. Arrays improve data organization and reduce code complexity.

### ▶ Characteristics of Arrays

- Arrays can store multiple values
- Values are stored using indexes
- Index numbering starts from 0
- Arrays can store numbers, strings and objects
- Arrays provide organized data storage.

### ▶ Structure of Array

In JavaScript, arrays are created using square brackets [ ]. Multiple values are stored inside brackets.

**Syntax**

var arrayName =

[value1, value2, value3];

**Example:**

var fruits =

["Apple", "Mango", "Orange"];

Here:

- Apple's index is 0
- Mango's index is 1
- Orange's index is 2

Each value is accessed using its index number.

### ▶ Accessing Array Elements

JavaScript uses index numbers to access values.

**Example**

var fruits =

["Apple", "Mango", "Orange"];

document.write(fruits[1]);

Output:

Mango

### ▶ Modifying Array Elements

Array values can also be changed dynamically.

**Example**

var fruits =

["Apple", "Mango", "Orange"];

fruits[0] = "Banana";

### ▶ Array Length Property

JavaScript provides the length property to determine the number of elements in an array.

**Example**

var fruits =

["Apple", "Mango", "Orange"];

document.write(fruits.length);

### ▶ Looping Through Arrays

Arrays are commonly used with loops for repeated processing.

**Example**

var fruits =

["Apple", "Mango", "Orange"];

for(var i = 0;

i < fruits.length;

```
i++) {
document.write(fruits[i]);
}
```

- **Advantages of Arrays**
  - It stores multiple values efficiently
  - It reduces number of variables
  - It simplifies data processing
  - It improves program organization
  - It works efficiently with loops

## 5.2 DOM Methods in JavaScript

Document Object Model, commonly called DOM. DOM methods allow JavaScript to communicate with HTML elements.

- **Definition of DOM**

DOM (Document Object Model) can be defined as a programming interface that represents an HTML document as a tree structure of objects. Each HTML element becomes an object that Java Script can access and manipulate.

DOM connects Java Script with HTML webpages.

Java Script requires a mechanism to:

- Access webpage elements
- Change content dynamically
- Modify styles
- Respond to user actions

DOM methods provide this capability.

- **DOM Tree Structure**

When a webpage loads, the browser converts the HTML document into a tree-like structure.

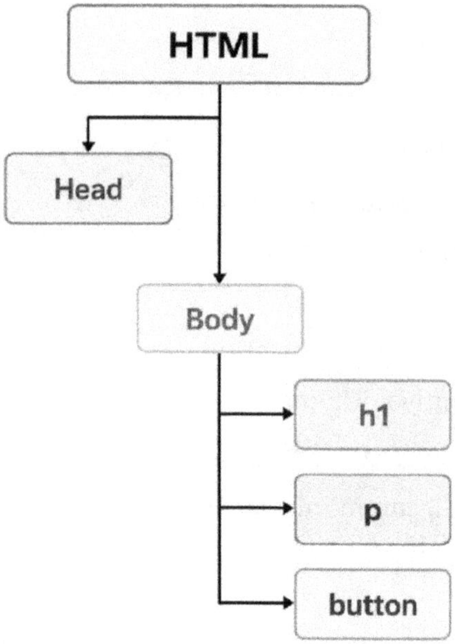


**Fig 5.1: DOM Tree Structure**

### ▶ Common DOM Methods

**1. getElementById():** This method selects an element using its unique id.

**Syntax**

document.getElementById("idName");

**Example**

document.getElementById("demo");

**2. getElementsByTagName():** This method selects elements based on their HTML tag name.

**Syntax**

document.getElementsByTagName("p");

**3. getElementsByClassName():** This method selects elements using class names.

**Syntax**

document.getElementsByClassName("text");

**4. querySelector():** This method selects the first matching CSS selector.

**Example**

document.querySelector(".box");

**5. querySelectorAll():** This method selects all matching CSS selector elements.

**Example**

```
document.querySelectorAll("p");
```

### ▶ Manipulating Elements Using DOM

DOM methods not only access elements but also modify them dynamically.

- **Changing Content:** webpage content changes dynamically.

**Example**

```
document.getElementById("demo").innerHTML = "Welcome";
```

- **Changing Styles:** element appearance can be modified dynamically.

**Example**

```
document.getElementById("demo").style.color = "red";
```

### ▶ Example

```
<!DOCTYPE html>
<html>
<body>
<h1 id="demo">
Hello
</h1>
<button onclick="changeText()">
Click Here
</button>
<script>
function changeText() {
document.getElementById("demo").innerHTML = "Welcome Student";
}
</script>
</body>
</html>
```

Output:

Here, a heading is created using HTML. JavaScript accesses the heading using getElementById(). When button is clicked, the text changes dynamically. DOM methods make webpages interactive.

### ▶ Applications of DOM Methods

DOM methods are widely used in:

- Dynamic content updates
- Form validation
- Interactive menus
- Animations
- Real-time notifications

### ▶ Advantages of DOM Methods

- It enables dynamic webpage updates
- It improves user interaction
- It supports real-time modifications and reduces webpage reloads
- It increases webpage responsiveness

## 5.3 Strings

Stringsare used to store and manipulate textual data. In programming, many applications require handling of text such as names, addresses, passwords, messages and emails.

JavaScript provides the string data type for storing sequences of characters. A string may contain letters, numbers, symbols or spaces enclosed within quotation marks.

### ▶ Definition of String

A string can be defined as a sequence of characters enclosed within single quotes (' '), double quotes (" ") or backticks (` `).

### ▶ Creating Strings

Strings can be created in different ways.

#### 1. Using Double Quotes

```
var name = "John";
```

#### 2. Using Single Quotes

```
var city = 'Hyderabad';
```

#### 3. Using Backticks

```
var msg = `Welcome Student`;
```

## ▶ String Operations

JavaScript provides various operations for handling strings.

### 1. String Concatenation

Concatenation means combining two or more strings.

**Example**

```
var first = "Hello";
var second = "Student";
var result =
first + " " + second;
document.write(result);
```

Output:

Hello Student

### 2. String Length

The length property returns the total number of characters in a string.

**Example**

```
var text = "JavaScript";
document.write(text.length);
```

### 3. Converting Case

JavaScript provides methods to change character case.

**Example**

```
toUpperCase()
var text = "hello";
document.write(
text.toUpperCase()
);
toLowerCase()
var text = "HELLO";
document.write(
text.toLowerCase()
);
```

### 4. Extracting Characters

JavaScript allows access to individual characters using index numbers.

**Example**

```
var text = "JavaScript";
document.write(text[0]);
```

Output:

J

## 5. Searching in Strings

JavaScript provides methods to search within strings.

**Example**

```
var text = "JavaScript";
document.write(
text.indexOf("Script")
);
```

▶ **Example**

```
<!DOCTYPE html>
<html>
<body>
<script>
var firstName = "Web";
var lastName = "Programming";
var fullName =
firstName + " " + lastName;
document.write(fullName);
</script>
</body>
</html>
```

Output:

Web Programming

Here, two strings are stored in variables. JavaScript combines them using concatenation. Full name is displayed as output

### Advantages of Strings

- It stores textual data efficiently
- It supports dynamic content generation
- It enables text manipulation
- It improves user interaction
- It supports searching and formatting

## 5.4 JavaScript Dialogue Boxes

JavaScript provides built-in dialogue boxes for this purpose. These dialogue boxes appear as popup windows in the browser and allow interaction with users.

### Definition of Dialogue Box

A dialogue box can be defined as a popup window displayed by JavaScript to interact with the user by showing messages, taking input or requesting confirmation.

### Types of Dialogue Boxes

JavaScript mainly provides three types of dialogue boxes:

1. Alert Box
2. Confirmation Box
3. Prompt Box

### 1. Alert Box

The alert box is used to display warning messages or information to the user. It contains a message and an OK button.Alert box provides simple notifications.

Alert boxes are used for:

- Success messages
- Warning notifications
- Error alerts

Example:

- "Login Successful"
- "Invalid Password"

**Syntax**

alert("Message");

**Example**

alert("Welcome to Web Programming");

## 2. Confirmation Box

The confirmation box is used when the webpage requires user confirmation before performing an action. It contains OK and Cancel buttons. It helps in decision-making.

Confirmation boxes are used in:

- Delete operations
- Logout confirmation
- Payment confirmation

**Syntax**

confirm("Message");

**Example**

confirm("Do you want to submit?");

## 3. Prompt Box

The prompt box is used to take input from the user through a text field. It contains a message, input box, OK button and Cancel button. Prompt boxes collect user data dynamically.

Prompt boxes are used in:

- Username input
- Search operations
- User personalization

**Syntax**

prompt("Message");

**Example**

prompt("Enter your name");

▶ **Example**

```
<!DOCTYPE html>
<html>
<body>
<script>
alert("Welcome Student");
confirm("Do you want to continue?");
var name =prompt("Enter your name");
document.write(name);
```

```
</script>
</body>
</html>
```

Output:

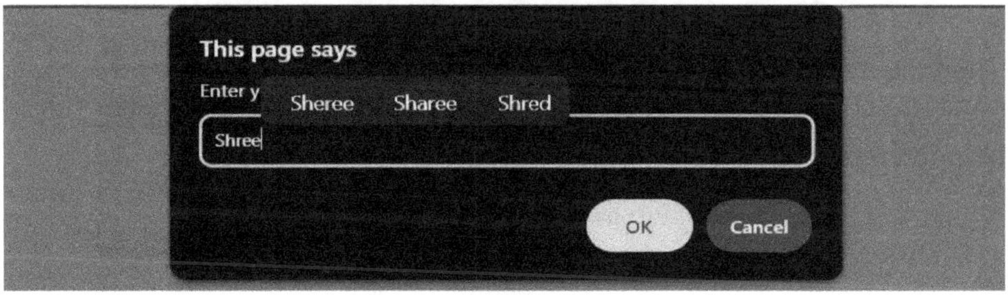


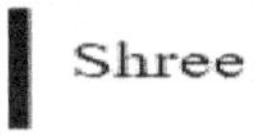


Here, alert box displays welcome message. Confirmation box asks user decision and prompt box collects user name. Entered name is displayed on webpage.

### ▶ Advantages of Dialogue Boxes

Dialogue boxes provide several advantages:

- It improves user interaction
- It provides instant feedback
- It collects user input
- It supports decision-making
- It increases webpage interactivity

## 5.5 Event Handling in JavaScript

User actions are called events, and JavaScript handles them using event handling mechanisms. Event handling allows webpages to react intelligently whenever an event occurs.

### ▶ Definition of Event

An event is defined as state change in an object and action or occurrence detected by the browser, such as mouse click, key press or webpage loading.

### ▶ Definition of Event Handling

Event handling can be defined as the process of detecting and responding to events using JavaScript code.

Event handling is required for:

- Button click actions
- Form validation
- Dynamic menus
- Keyboard interaction
- Interactive animations

### ▶ Types of Events

JavaScript supports different categories of events.

**1. Mouse Events**: Mouse events occur when users interact with webpage elements using the mouse. Mouse events support graphical interaction.

**Common Mouse Events**

| Event | Purpose |
|---|---|
| onclick | when mouse click on an element |
| ondblclick | Triggers on double click |
| onmouseover | Triggers when mouse enters element |
| onmouseout | Triggers when mouse leaves element |
| onmousedown | Pressed over the element |
| onmouseup | Released over the element |
| onmousemove | When mouse movement takes place |

**Example**

```
<button onclick="showMessage()">
Click Me
</button>
<script>
function showMessage() {
```

```
  alert("Button Clicked");
}
</script>
```

Output:

**2. Keyboard Events:** Keyboard events occur when users press or release keys on the keyboard. Keyboard events support typing interaction.

**Common Keyboard Events**

| Event | Purpose |
|---|---|
| onkeydown | Triggers when key is pressed |
| onkeyup | Triggers when key is released |
| onkeypress | Triggers while pressing key |

**Example**

```
<input type="text"
onkeyup="showText()">
<script>
function showText() {
  alert("Key Released");
}
</script>
```

**3. Window Events:** Window events occur due to browser window activities such as loading or resizing webpages. Window events control browser-level interactions.

**Common Window Events**

| Event | Purpose |
|---|---|
| onload | Triggers when webpage loads |
| onresize | Triggers when window resizes |
| onscroll | Triggers during scrolling |
| onunload | Triggers when the visitor leaves the current webpage the browser unloads it |

**Example**

```
<body onload="welcome()">
<script>
function welcome() {
  alert("Page Loaded");
}
</script>
```

- **Advantages of Event Handling**
    - It improves interactivity
    - It supports dynamic webpages
    - It enhances user experience
    - It enables real-time response
    - It simplifies user communication

## 5.6 Introduction to XML

### XML Basics

XML stands for ExtensibleMarkupLanguage.

It is designed for the describing the data in a plain text format.

XML is designed specifically for storing, organizing and transporting data in a structured format.

XML was created in the year 1998 (version 1.0).

## ▶ Definition of XML

XML (Extensible Markup Language) can be defined as a markup language used to store, organize and transport data in a structured and self-descriptive format.

XML is called extensible because in XML, users can create their owntags according to application requirements.

XML is easy and fast processing data compared to HTML.

For example:

<student>

<name>Ann</name>

</student>

Here:

- <student> and <name> are custom tags created by the user.

## ▶ Features of XML

**1. Extensible:** Users can create custom tags.XML provides flexibility.

**2. Self-Descriptive:** Tags describe the meaning of data.XML improves readability.

**3. Platform Independent:** XML can be used across different operating systems and programming languages.

**4. Structured Format:** Data is organized hierarchically using parent-child relationships.

**5. Human Readable:** XML documents are easy to read and understand.

**6. Separatesthedata:** Describing the data in XML is unique compared to remaining languages because XML data can be used by different programming languages whereas HTML cannot do separation of data in plain text format.

## ▶ Structure of XML Document

An XML document contains:

- Declaration
- Root element
- Child elements
- Closing tags

Thus, XML follows a hierarchical tree structure.

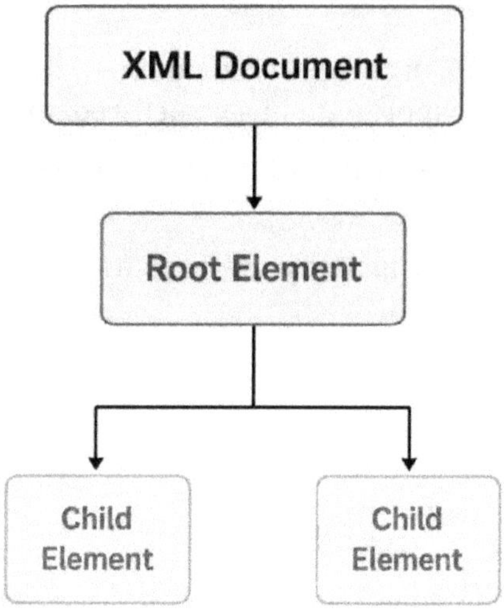


**Fig 5.2: Structure of XML Document**

▶ **Basic Rules of XML**

**1. Every Tag Must Be Closed:** Opening and closing tags are mandatory.

**Example:**

<name>Life</name>

**2. Tags Are Case Sensitive:** XML distinguishes uppercase and lowercase.

<Name>Jaya</Name>is different from<name>Jaya</name>

**3. Proper Nesting Is Required:** Elements must be nested correctly.

**Example:**

```
<student>
<name>Jyo</name>
</student>
```

**4. XML Must Have One Root Element:** Every XML document must contain a single root element.So, that XML maintains hierarchical structure.

▶ **Example**

```
<?xml version="1.0"?>
<student>
<name>Jaya</name>
<course>BSc MS CS</course>
<college>OU</college>
</student>
```

Here, in the example,

- <?xml version="1.0"?> is XML declaration.
- <student> is root element.
- <name>, <course>, <college> are child elements storing data.

### ▶ Applications of XML

XML is widely used in:

- Web services
- Data storage
- Configuration files
- Database exchange
- APIs
- Online applications

For example, many software systems exchange information using XML documents.

## Advantages of XML

XML provides several advantages:

- It stores structured data
- It supports data exchange
- It is platform independent
- It is human readable
- It is extensible and flexible

### Difference Between HTML and XML

| Aspect | HTML | XML |
|---|---|---|
| Purpose | Display data | Store and transport data |
| Tags | Predefined | User-defined |
| Focus | Presentation | Data structure |
| Extensibility | Limited | Highly extensible |
| Case sensitivity | Not case sensitive | Case sensitive |
| Data Processing | Slow | Fast |

## 5.7 Structuring Data

If data is stored without proper structure, it becomes difficult to read, search and manage. XML solves this problem by organizing information in a hierarchical format using elements and tags.

## ▶ Definition

Structuring data can be defined as the process of organizing information in a logical and hierarchical format using XML elements and tags.

XML provides structured representation that makes data easy to manage and exchange.

## ▶ Hierarchical Structure in XML

XML organizes data using a hierarchical parent-child relationship.

The structure usually contains:

- Root element
- Parent elements
- Child elements

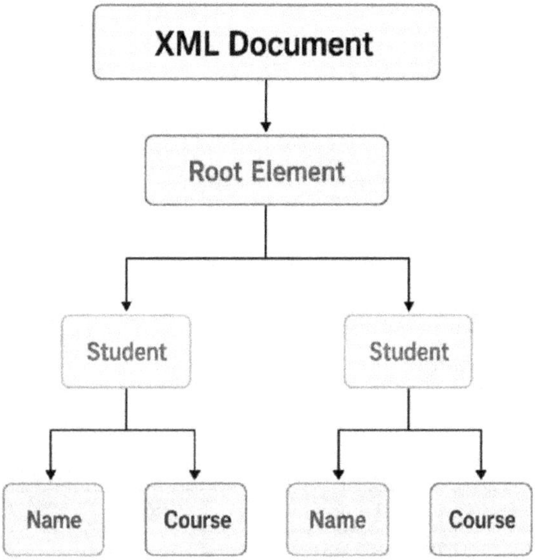


**Fig 5.3: Hierarchical Structure of XML Data**

1. **Root Element:** The root element is the main element that contains all other elements in the XML document. Every XML document must contain only one root element.
2. **Child Elements:** Child elements are elements placed inside another element. They store detailed information related to the parent element. It helpsinorganize data logically.

## ▶ Example of Structured XML Data

```
<?xml version="1.0"?>

<college>

<student>
```

```
<name>Jaya</name>
<course>BSc MS CS</course>
<year>3rd Year</year>
</student>
<student>
<name>Ravi</name>
<course>BCA</course>
<year>2nd Year</year>
</student>
</college>
```

Here, <college> is root element, <student> is parent element and <name>, <course>, <year> are child elements storing student information

### ▶ Features of Structured XML Data

**1. Organized Representation:** Data is arranged systematically using elements and tags.

**2. Easy Data Exchange:** Applications can exchange structured XML documents easily.

**3. Flexible Structure:** Users can create custom elements according to requirements.

**4. Readability:** XML structure is human readable and easy to interpret. Maintenance becomes simpler.

## 5.8 Document Type Definition (DTD) and Its Types

XML allows users to create custom tags, but if there are no rules, different XML documents may follow different structures, leading to inconsistency and errors.

A DTD defines the legal structure, elements and rules of an XML document.

It ensures that the XML document follows a valid format.

### ▶ Definition

Document Type Definition (DTD) can be defined as a set of rules that defines the structure, elements and attributes allowed in an XML document.

Without DTD, XML documents may contain invalid elements and structure may become inconsistent. DTD provides rules for validation and consistency.

### ▶ Functions of DTD

- It defines valid XML elements
- It specifies parent-child relationships
- It defines attributes

- It ensures proper XML structure
- It validates XML documents

### Structure of DTD

DTD declarations are written using <!DOCTYPE> syntax.

### Example

```
<!DOCTYPE student [
<!ELEMENT student (name, course)>
<!ELEMENT name (#PCDATA)>
<!ELEMENT course (#PCDATA)>
]>
```

Here, <!DOCTYPE student> defines root element, <!ELEMENT student (name, course)> defines student element must contain name and course and #PCDATA is parsed character data (text content)

Thus, DTD specifies XML structure clearly.

### Types of DTD

DTD rules can be written inside or outside the XML document. DTD is mainly divided into two types:

1. Internal DTD
2. External DTD

**1. Internal DTD**: Internal DTD is a type of DTD where the DTD rules are written inside the same XML document. Structure and data remain together in one file.

**Example**

```
<?xml version="1.0"?>
<!DOCTYPE student [
<!ELEMENT student (name, course)>
<!ELEMENT name (#PCDATA)>
<!ELEMENT course (#PCDATA)>
]>
<student>
<name>Vidya</name>
<course>BTech AIML</course>
</student>
```

The browser or XML parser reads the DTD rules from within the XML file and validates the document accordingly.

## Advantages of Internal DTD

- It is easy to manage for small documents
- There is no separate DTD file required
- It is suitable for simple XML structures

**2. External DTD:** External DTD is a type of DTD where the DTD rules are stored in a separate .dtd file and linked to the XML document. **V**alidation rules are maintained externally.

**Example**

- **XML File**

```
<?xml version="1.0"?>
<!DOCTYPE student SYSTEM "student.dtd">
<student>
<name>Vidya</name>
<course>BTech AIML</course>
</student>
```

- **DTD File (student.dtd)**

```
<!ELEMENT student (name, course)>
<!ELEMENT name (#PCDATA)>
<!ELEMENT course (#PCDATA)>
```

- **Advantages of External DTD**
  - It is reusable across multiple XML files
  - It's easy maintenance
  - It is suitable for large systems.

- **Advantages of DTD**
  - It ensures valid XML structure
  - It improves consistency
  - It prevents invalid data
  - It simplifies XML validation
  - It supports standardized communication.

## 5.9 XML Namespaces

- Namespaces uniquely identify elements and prevent naming conflicts. XML namespaces improve clarity and organization in XML documents.
- Suppose two XML documents contain the same element name <table>, but one represents a furniture table and the other represents a database table.

- Without namespaces, the XML parser cannot distinguish between them. Namespaces provide unique identification and remove doubt.

### Definition

An XML Namespace can be defined as a method used to uniquely identify XML elements and attributes by associating them with a specific name or URI.

**Example**

```
<table>
<name>Wooden Table</name>
</table>
<table>
<name>Student Data</name>
</table>
```

Here, both use the same tag <table> and meaning becomes confusing.

### Syntax of Namespace

Namespaces are declared using the xmlns attribute.

**Syntax**

```
xmlns:prefix="URI"
```

Where, xmlns is namespace declaration, prefix is namespace identifier and URI is Unique resource identifier

### Example

```
<root
xmlns:f="http://furniture.com"
xmlns:s="http://student.com">
<f:table>
<f:name>Wooden Table</f:name>
</f:table>
<s:table>
<s:name>Student Record</s:name>
</s:table>
</root>
```

Here, xmlns:f is namespace for furniture data

- xmlns:s is namespace for student data
- f:table is furniture table
- s:table is student table

## ▶ Types of XML Namespaces

Namespaces can be declared with or without prefixes. XML mainly supports:

- Default Namespace
- Prefixed Namespace

**1. Default Namespace**: In default namespace, elements use a namespace without prefixes.

**Example**

```
<book
xmlns="http://books.com">
<title>XML Basics</title>
</book>
```

**2. Prefixed Namespace:** In prefixed namespace, prefixes are attached to element names.

**Example**

```
<h:table
xmlns:h="http://html.com">
<h:tr>
<h:td>Data</h:td>
</h:tr>
</h:table>
```

## ▶ Advantages of XML Namespaces

- It prevents naming conflicts
- It improves data clarity
- It supports integration of multiple XML documents
- It enables unique identification
- It improves interoperability

## ▶ Difference Between XML Tags with and Without Namespace

| Aspect | Without Namespace | With Namespace |
|---|---|---|
| Identification | Ambiguous | Unique |
| Conflict Handling | Difficult | Easy |
| Data Clarity | Less | More |
| Usage | Simple systems | Large systems |

## 5.10 XML DOM

XML DOM stands for XML Document Object Model.

In XML applications, data is stored in a structured format using elements and tags.

XML DOM represents the XML document as a tree structure where every element becomes an object that can be accessed and manipulated programmatically

XML documents may contain large amounts of structured data. Applications must:

- Read XML data
- Modify elements
- Add new data
- Delete existing data

Without XML DOM, manipulating XML documents dynamically would become difficult.

- **Definition:** XML DOM (Document Object Model) can be defined as a programming interface that represents an XML document as a tree structure of objects, allowing programs to access and manipulate XML data dynamically

### Structure of XML DOM

In XML DOM, every part of the XML document becomes a node.

Types of nodes:

- Root node
- Element nodes
- Text nodes
- Attribute nodes

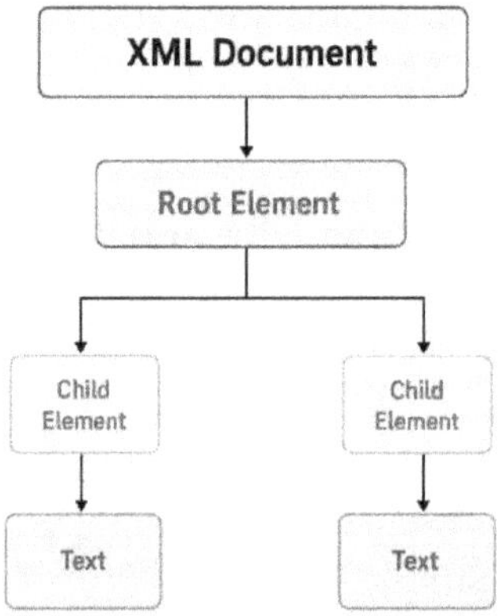


**Fig 5.4: XML DOM Tree Structure**

- **XML DOM Node Relationships:** XML DOM follows hierarchical relationships.
    - Parent Node
    - Child Node
    - Sibling Node

**Example**

```
<student>
<name>Jaya</name>
<course>BSc MS CS</course>
</student>
```

Here, <student> is parent node, <name> and <course> are child nodes.

### ▶ Accessing XML Elements Using DOM

XML DOM provides methods to access elements dynamically.

**1. getElementsByTagName():** It is used to access elements using tag names.

**Example:** `xmlDoc.getElementsByTagName("name");`

**2. Accessing Node Value:** It is used to retrieve text stored inside elements.

**Example:**

```
xmlDoc
.getElementsByTagName("name")[0]
.childNodes[0]
.nodeValue;
```

### ▶ Modifying XML Data Using DOM

XML DOM allows modification of XML elements.

**Example**

```
xmlDoc
.getElementsByTagName("name")[0]
.childNodes[0]
.nodeValue = "Ram";
```

**Example**

```
<student>
<name>Ram</name>
<course>BTech CSE</course>
</student>
```

### JavaScript DOM Access

```
var x =
xmlDoc.getElementsByTagName("name")[0]
.childNodes[0]
.nodeValue;
document.write(x);
```

Output:

Ram

### Advantages of XML DOM

- It provides dynamic manipulation of XML.
- It provides structured data access
- It is easy navigation through nodes
- It supports updating and deleting data
- It is platform independent
- It improves XML processing efficiency.

### Difference Between XML and XML DOM

| Aspect | XML | XML DOM |
|---|---|---|
| Purpose | Store data | Access and manipulate data |
| Structure | Static document | Dynamic object model |
| Functionality | Data representation | Data processing |
| Interaction | Limited | Dynamic manipulation |

# Module: VI

# Overview of PHP

## 6.1 General Syntactic Characteristics Primitive

PHP stands for Hypertext Preprocessor. It is object-oriented scripting language that can be executed at the server-side. PHP is well suited for web development.

PHP was created by Rasmus Lerdorf in 1994 but appeared in the market in 1995.

PHP 7.4.0 is the latest version of PHP, which was released on 28 November.

### Features:

1. PHP is an interpreted language, i.e., there is no need for compilation.
2. PHP is faster than other scripting languages, for example, ASP and JSP.
3. PHP is a server-side scripting language, which is used to manage the dynamic content of the website.
4. PHP can be embedded into HTML.
5. PHP is an object-oriented language.
6. PHP is an open-source scripting language.
7. PHP is simple and easy to learn language.
8. PHP can handle the forms, such as - collect the data from users using forms, save it into the database, and return useful information to the user. For example - Registration form.
9. PHP has easily understandable syntax. Programmers are comfortable coding with it.
10. PHP code can be easily embedded within HTML tags and script.
11. PHP is a secure language to develop the website. It consists of multiple layers of security to prevent threads and malicious attacks.
12. PHP has predefined error reporting constants to generate an error notice or warning at runtime. E.g., E_ERROR, E_WARNING, E_STRICT, E_PARSE.
13. It has a large community of developers who regularly updates documentation, tutorials, online help, and FAQs.

## PHP Echo and Print

### ▶ PHP Echo

PHP echo is a language construct used to display output on the screen. It is not a function, so parentheses are not compulsory. However, parentheses are required when more than one parameter is used.

### ▶ Syntax

echo "message";

or

echo("message");

### ▶ Important Points about Echo

- echo is used to display output.
- Parentheses are optional.
- It does not return any value.
- Multiple strings can be passed using commas.
- echo executes faster than print.

### ▶ Printing a String using Echo

**Example**

```
<?php
echo "Hello by PHP echo";
?>
```

Output

Hello by PHP echo

### ▶ Printing Multi-line String using Echo

**Example**

```
<?php
echo "Hello by PHP echo
this is multi line
text printed by
PHP echo statement";
?>
```

Output

Hello by PHP echo this is multi line text printed by PHP echo statement

### ▶ Printing Escaping Characters using Echo

**Program**

```
<?php
echo "Hello escape \"sequence\" characters";
?>
```

Output

Hello escape "sequence" characters

### ▶ Printing Variable Value using Echo

**Example**

```
<?php
$msg="Hello JavaTpoint PHP";
echo "Message is: $msg";
?>
```

Output

Message is: Hello JavaTpoint PHP

### ▶ PHP Print

PHP print is also a language construct used to display output. Parentheses are optional. Unlike echo, print always returns the value 1.

### ▶ Syntax

```
print "message";
```

or

```
print("message");
```

### ▶ Important Points about Print

- print is used to display output.
- Parentheses are optional.
- It always returns integer value 1.
- Multiple arguments cannot be passed.
- print is slower than echo.

### ▶ Printing a String using Print

**Example**

```
<?php
print "Hello by PHP print ";
print ("Hello by PHP print()");
```

```
?>
```

Output

Hello by PHP print Hello by PHP print()

### ▶ Printing Multi-line String using Print

**Example**

```
<?php
print "Hello by PHP print
this is multi line
text printed by
PHP print statement";
?>
```

Output

Hello by PHP print this is multi line text printed by PHP print statement

### ▶ Printing Escaping Characters using Print

**Example**

```
<?php
print "Hello escape \"sequence\" characters by PHP print";
?>
```

Output

Hello escape "sequence" characters by PHP print

### ▶ Printing Variable Value using Print

**Example**

```
<?php
$msg="Hello print() in PHP";
print "Message is: $msg";
?>
```

Output

Message is: Hello print() in PHP

### ▶ Difference Between Echo and Print

| Echo | Print |
|---|---|
| echo is used to display output. | print is also used to display output. |
| Parentheses are optional. | Parentheses are optional. |

| | |
|---|---|
| echo does not return any value. | print always returns 1. |
| Multiple arguments can be passed. | Multiple arguments cannot be passed. |
| Faster than print. | Slower than echo. |

## PHP Variables

In PHP, a variable is declared using the dollar ($) symbol followed by the variable name. Variables are used to store data values such as strings, integers, and floating-point numbers.

### ▶ Important Points about PHP Variables

- PHP is a loosely typed language, so there is no need to declare the datatype of a variable.
- PHP automatically converts the variable into the appropriate datatype.
- Variables can be reused throughout the program.
- Assignment operator (=) is used to assign values to variables.
- Variable names are case-sensitive.

### ▶ Syntax of PHP Variable

```
$variablename = value;
```

Example:

```
$name = "PHP";
```

### ▶ Rules for Declaring PHP Variables

- Variable must start with a dollar ($) symbol.
- Variable name must begin with a letter or underscore (_).
- Variable can contain alphabets, numbers, and underscore.
- Variable names cannot contain spaces.
- Variable names cannot start with numbers or special symbols.
- Variable names are case-sensitive.

### ▶ Declaring String, Integer, and Float Variables

**Example**

```
<?php
$str="hello string";
$x=200;
$y=44.6;
echo "string is: $str <br/>";
echo "integer is: $x <br/>";
```

```
echo "float is: $y <br/>";
?>
```

Output

string is: hello string

integer is: 200

float is: 44.6

## ▶ Case Sensitive Variables

In PHP, variable names are case-sensitive. Therefore $color, $COLOR, and $coLOR are treated as different variables.

### Example

```
<?php
$color="red";
echo "My car is " . $color . "<br>";
echo "My house is " . $COLOR . "<br>";
echo "My boat is " . $coLOR . "<br>";
?>
```

Output:

My car is red

Notice: Undefined variable: COLOR

My house is

Notice: Undefined variable: coLOR

My boat is

## ▶ Valid and Invalid Variables

### Valid Variables

Example

```
<?php
$a="hello";
$_b="hello";
echo "$a <br/> $_b";
?>
```

Output

hello

hello

**Invalid Variables**

Example

```
<?php
$4c="hello";
$*d="hello";
echo "$4c <br/> $*d";
?>
```

Output

Parse error: syntax error

### ▶ PHP as a Loosely Typed Language

PHP is called a loosely typed language because it automatically converts variables into the correct datatype according to the assigned value.

Example:

```
<?php
$x = 10;
$y = "20";
echo $x + $y;
?>
```

Output:

30

### ▶ PHP Variable Scope

Variable scope defines the area of the program where a variable can be accessed.

PHP supports three types of variable scope:

1. Local Variable
2. Global Variable
3. Static Variable

### ▶ Local Variable

A variable declared inside a function is called a local variable. It can only be accessed within that function.

## Program

```
<?php
function local_var()
{
```

```
    $num = 55;
    echo "Local variable declared inside the function is: ".$num;
}
local_var();
?>
```

Output

Local variable declared inside the function is: 55

### ▶ Global Variable

A variable declared outside the function is called a global variable. To access it inside a function, the global keyword is used.

**Program**

```
<?php
$name = "Sanaya Sharma";
function global_var()
{
    global $name;
    echo "Variable inside the function: ".$name;
    echo "</br>";
}
global_var();
echo "Variable outside the function: ".$name;
?>
```

Output

Variable inside the function: Sanaya Sharma

Variable outside the function: Sanaya Sharma

## Using $GLOBALS Array

PHP provides a predefined $GLOBALS array to access global variables inside a function.

**Program**

```
<?php
$num1 = 5;
$num2 = 13;
function global_var()
```

```
{
  $sum = $GLOBALS['num1'] + $GLOBALS['num2'];
  echo "Sum of global variables is: ".$sum;
}
global_var();
?>
```

Output

Sum of global variables is: 18

### ▶ Local Variable Priority over Global Variable

If local and global variables have the same name, then the local variable gets higher priority inside the function.

**Program**

```
<?php
$x = 5;
function mytest()
{
  $x = 10;
  echo "Value of x: ".$x;
}
mytest();
?>
```

Output

Value of x: 10

### ▶ Static Variable

Normally, variables are destroyed after function execution completes. To preserve the variable value between function calls, PHP uses static variables.

Static variables are declared using the static keyword.

**Program**

```
<?php
function static_var()
{static $num1 = 3;
$num2 = 6;
  $num1++;
```

```
  $num2++;
echo "Static: ".$num1."</br>";
  echo "Non-static: ".$num2."</br>";
}
static_var();
static_var();
?>
```

Output

Static: 4

Non-static: 7

Static: 5

Non-static: 7

## PHP Constants

PHP constants are identifiers whose values cannot be changed during the execution of the program. Once a constant is defined, it remains fixed throughout the script except for magic constants.

Constants can be created in two ways:

1. Using define() function
2. Using const keyword

Constants are similar to variables, but their values cannot be modified or undefined once assigned.

Conventionally, constants are written in uppercase letters.

Unlike variables, constants are automatically global throughout the script.

### ▶ Defining Constants using define()

The define() function is used to create constants at runtime.

### ▶ Syntax

define(name, value, case-insensitive);

### ▶ Parameters

- Name: Specifies the constant name.
- Value: Specifies the constant value.
- case-insensitive: Specifies whether the constant is case-insensitive. Default value is false.

### ▶ Example of define()

**Example**

```
<?php
define("MESSAGE","Hello");
echo MESSAGE;
?>
```

Output

Hello

### ▶ Case-Insensitive Constant

**Program**

```
<?php
define("MESSAGE","Hello", true);
echo MESSAGE, "</br>";
echo message;
?>
```

Output

Hello

Hello

### ▶ Case-Sensitive Constant

**Program**

```
<?php
define("MESSAGE","Helloclass", false);
echo MESSAGE;
echo message;
?>
```

Output

Hello class

### ▶ Defining Constants using const Keyword

PHP provides the const keyword to create constants at compile time. It is a language construct and not a function.

Constants declared using const are always case-sensitive.

**Program**

```
<?php
const MESSAGE = "Hello PHP";
echo MESSAGE;
?>
```

Output

Hello PHP

### ▶ constant() Function

The constant() function is another method used to print the value of a constant.

▶ **Syntax:** constant(name);

### ▶ Example of constant() Function

**Program**

```
<?php
define("MSG", "PHP");
echo MSG, "</br>";
echo constant("MSG");
?>
```

Output

PHP

PHP

### ▶ Difference Between Constants and Variables

| Constants | Variables |
|---|---|
| Once defined, constants cannot be changed or redefined. | Variables can be changed or redefined easily. |
| Constants are defined using define() or const. | Variables are defined using assignment operator (=). |
| No dollar ($) symbol is used before constants. | Variables always use dollar ($) symbol. |
| Constants do not follow variable scoping rules. | Variables follow scope rules such as local, global, and static scope. |
| Constant values remain fixed throughout the program. | Variable values can change during execution. |
| Constants are global by default. | Variables may be local, global, or static. |

## PHP Data Types

PHP data types are used to store different kinds of values or data. PHP supports 8 primitive data types, which are categorized into three groups:

### 1. Scalar Types

Scalar data types hold only a single value.

PHP provides four scalar data types:

- Boolean
- Integer
- Float
- String

### 2. Compound Types

Compound data types can store multiple values.

PHP provides two compound data types:

- Array
- Object

### 3. Special Types

PHP provides two special data types:

- Resource
- NULL

### ▶ PHP Boolean

Boolean is the simplest data type in PHP. It works like a switch and stores only two possible values:

- TRUE (1)
- FALSE (0)

Boolean values are mostly used in conditional statements.

### ▶ Example of Boolean

**Program**

```
<?php
if (TRUE)
  echo "This condition is TRUE.";
if (FALSE)
  echo "This condition is FALSE.";
?>
```

Output

This condition is TRUE.

### ▶ PHP Integer

Integer is a numeric data type that stores whole numbers without decimal points. Integers may be positive or negative.

### ▶ Rules for Integer

- Integer can be positive or negative.
- Integer must not contain decimal points.
- Integer may be:
  - Decimal (Base 10)
  - Octal (Base 8)
  - Hexadecimal (Base 16)
- Integer range lies between:
  - $-2^{31}$ to $2^{31}$

### ▶ Example of Integer

```
<?php
$dec1 = 34;
$oct1 = 0243;
$hexa1 = 0x45;
echo "Decimal number: ".$dec1."</br>";
echo "Octal number: ".$oct1."</br>";
echo "HexaDecimal number: ".$hexa1."</br>";
?>
```

Output

Decimal number: 34

Octal number: 163

HexaDecimal number: 69

### ▶ PHP Float

Float is a data type that stores numbers containing decimal or fractional values. It may contain positive or negative decimal numbers.

### ▶ Example of Float

```
<?php
$n1 = 19.34;
```

```
$n2 = 54.472;
$sum = $n1 + $n2;
echo "Addition of floating numbers: ".$sum;
?>
```

Output

Addition of floating numbers: 73.812

### ▶ PHP String

String is a non-numeric data type used to store text, alphabets, numbers, and special characters.

Strings can be enclosed in:

- Double quotes (" ")
- Single quotes (' ')

Both behave differently in PHP.

### ▶ Example of String

```
<?php
$company = "World";
//Double quote
echo "Hello $company";
echo "</br>";
//Single quote
echo 'Hello $company';
?>
```

Output

Hello World

Hello $company

### ▶ Compound Data Types

**Array:** An array stores multiple values in a single variable.

Example:

```
<?php
$colors = array("Red", "Green", "Blue");
echo $colors[0];
?>
```

Output

Red

**Object**: Object is an instance of a class that contains properties and methods.

Example:

```
<?php
class Student
{
  public $name = "Vidya";
}
$obj = new Student();
echo $obj->name;
?>
```

Output

Vidya

### ▶ Special Data Types

**Resource:** Resource is a special variable used to store references to external resources such as database connections or files.

Example:

```
<?php
$file = fopen("test.txt", "r");
?>
```

**NULL:** NULL represents a variable with no value assigned.

Example:

```
<?php
$x = NULL;
var_dump($x);
?>
```

Output

NULL

## PHP Comments

PHP comments can be used to describe any line of code so that other developer can understand the code easily.

It can also be used to hide any code.

PHP supports single line and multi-line comments.

These comments are similar to C/C++ and Perl style (Unix shell style) comments.

### ▶ PHP Single LineComments:

There are two ways to use single line comments in PHP.

- // (C++ style single line comment)
- # (Unix Shell style single line comment)

## 6.2 Operation and Expressions Output

### PHP Operators

PHP operators are symbols used to perform operations on variables and values. Operators help in performing mathematical calculations, comparisons, logical operations, string operations, and many other tasks.

Example:

```
<?php
$num = 10 + 20;
?>
```

Here:

- + is the operator
- 10 and 20 are operands
- $num stores the result

### ▶ Types of PHP Operators

PHP operators are categorized into the following types:

1. Arithmetic Operators
2. Assignment Operators
3. Bitwise Operators
4. Comparison Operators
5. Incrementing/Decrementing Operators
6. Logical Operators
7. String Operators
8. Array Operators
9. Type Operators
10. Execution Operators
11. Error Control Operator

### ▶ Classification Based on Operands

i) **Unary Operators:** Unary operators work on a single operand.

Examples:

- ++
- --

ii) **Binary Operators:** Binary operators work on two operands.

Examples:

- +
- -
- *
- /

iii) **Ternary Operators:** Ternary operators work on three operands.

Example:

- ?:

▶ **Arithmetic Operators:** Arithmetic operators are used to perform mathematical operations.

| Operator | Name | **Example** | **Description** |
|---|---|---|---|
| + | Addition | $a + $b | Adds two operands |
| - | Subtraction | $a - $b | Subtracts operands |
| * | Multiplication | $a * $b | Multiplies operands |
| / | Division | $a / $b | Divides operands |
| % | Modulus | $a % $b | Returns remainder |
| ** | Exponentiation | $a ** $b | Raises $a to power $b |

**Example**

```
<?php
$a = 10;
$b = 5;
echo $a + $b;
echo "</br>";
echo $a - $b;
echo "</br>";
echo $a * $b;
echo "</br>";
```

```
echo $a / $b;
?>
```

Output

```
15
5
50
2
```

- **Assignment Operators:** These operators are used to assign values to variables.

| Operator | Name | Example | Description |
|---|---|---|---|
| = | Assign | $a = $b | Assigns value |
| += | Add and Assign | $a += $b | Adds then assigns |
| -= | Subtract and Assign | $a -= $b | Subtracts then assigns |
| *= | Multiply and Assign | $a *= $b | Multiplies then assigns |
| /= | Divide and Assign | $a /= $b | Divides then assigns |
| %= | Modulus and Assign | $a %= $b | Finds remainder then assigns |

**Example**

```
<?php
$a = 10;
$a += 5;
echo $a;
?>
```

Output

```
15
```

- **Bitwise Operators:** These operators perform operations on bits.

| Operator | Name | Example |
|---|---|---|
| & | AND | $a & $b |
| ` | ` | OR |
| ^ | XOR | $a ^ $b |
| ~ | NOT | ~$a |
| << | Left Shift | $a << $b |
| >> | Right Shift | $a >> $b |

- **Comparison Operators:** Comparison operators compare two values.

| Operator | Name | Description |
|---|---|---|
| == | Equal | TRUE if values are equal |
| === | Identical | TRUE if values and datatype are same |
| != | Not Equal | TRUE if values are different |
| !== | Not Identical | TRUE if value or datatype differs |
| < | Less Than | TRUE if left value is smaller |
| > | Greater Than | TRUE if left value is greater |
| <= | Less Than or Equal | TRUE if smaller or equal |
| >= | Greater Than or Equal | TRUE if greater or equal |
| <=> | Spaceship | Returns -1, 0, or 1 |

**Example**

```
<?php
$a = 10;
$b = 20;
var_dump($a < $b);
?>
```

Output

```
bool(true)
```

- **Increment and Decrement Operators:** These operators increase or decrease variable values.

| Operator | Name | Description |
|---|---|---|
| ++$a | Pre Increment | Increment then return |
| $a++ | Post Increment | Return then increment |
| --$a | Pre Decrement | Decrement then return |
| $a-- | Post Decrement | Return then decrement |

**Example**

```
<?php
$a = 5;
echo ++$a;
?>
```

Output

```
6
```

- **Logical Operators:** These operators are used with conditional statements.

| **Operator** | **Name** | **Description** |
|---|---|---|
| and | AND | TRUE if both are true |
| or | OR | TRUE if either is true |
| xor | XOR | TRUE if only one is true |
| ! | NOT | Reverses result |
| && | AND | TRUE if both are true |

**Example**

```
<?php
$a = true;
$b = false;
var_dump($a && $b);
?>
```

Output

bool(false)

- **String Operators:** String operators work on strings.

| Operator | Name | **Description** |
|---|---|---|
| . | Concatenation | Combines strings |
| .= | Concatenate and Assign | Combines and assigns |

**Example**

```
<?php
$a = "Hello";
$b = " PHP";
echo $a . $b;
?>
```

Output

Hello PHP

- **Array Operators:** Array operators compare arrays.

| **Operator** | **Name** | **Description** |
|---|---|---|
| + | Union | Combines arrays |
| == | Equality | Same key/value pairs |
| != | Inequality | Arrays not equal |
| === | Identity | Same key/value and order |
| !== | Non-Identity | Arrays not identical |

- **Type Operator:** PHP uses instanceof operator to check object type.

**Example**

```
<?php
class Developer {}
$charu = new Developer();
var_dump($charuinstanceof Developer);
?>
```

Output

bool(true)

- **Execution Operator:** PHP provides backticks (``) as execution operator.

It executes shell commands.

**Example**

```
<?php
echo `dir`;
?>
```

- **Error Control Operator:** PHP uses @ symbol to suppress error messages.

**Example**

```
<?php
@file('non_existent_file');
?>
```

## 6.3 Control Statements

### PHP Conditional Statements and Loops

PHP provides conditional statements and looping statements to control the flow of program execution.

These statements help in decision making and repeated execution of code blocks.

- **PHP If Else Statements:** PHP provides different types of conditional statements:
    1. if statement
    2. if-else statement
    3. if-else-if statement
    4. nested if statement
- **PHP If Statement:** The if statement executes a block of code only when the specified condition is true.

- **Syntax**

```
if(condition){
  //code to be executed
}
```

**Example**

```
<?php
$num = 12;
if($num< 100){
  echo "$num is less than 100";
}
?>
```

Output

12 is less than 100

- **PHP If-Else Statement:** The if-else statement executes one block if the condition is true and another block if the condition is false.

- **Syntax**

```
if(condition){
  //code if condition is true
}
else{
  //code if condition is false
}
```

**Example**

```
<?php
$num = 12;
if($num % 2 == 0){
  echo "$num is even number";
}
else{
  echo "$num is odd number";
}
?>
```

Output

12 is even number

- **PHP If-Else-If Statement:** The if-else-if statement is used to test multiple conditions.
- **Syntax**

```
if(condition1){
  //code
}
elseif(condition2){
  //code
}
else{
  //code
}
```

**Example**

```
<?php
$marks = 69;
if($marks < 33){
  echo "Fail";
}
else if($marks >= 34 && $marks < 50){
  echo "D Grade";
}
else if($marks >= 50 && $marks < 65){
  echo "C Grade";
}
else if($marks >= 65 && $marks < 80){
  echo "B Grade";
}
else{
  echo "A Grade";
}
```

```
?>
```

Output

B Grade

- **PHP Nested If Statement:** Nested if means using an if statement inside another if statement.
- **Syntax**

```
if(condition){
  if(condition){
    //code
  }}
```

**Example**

```
<?php
$age = 23;
$nationality = "Indian";
if($nationality == "Indian"){
  if($age >= 18){
    echo "Eligible to give vote";
  }
  else{
    echo "Not eligible to give vote";
  }}
?>
```

Output

Eligible to give vote

- **PHP Switch Statement:** The switch statement is used to execute one statement from multiple conditions.
- **Syntax**

```
switch(expression){
  case value1:
    //code
    break;
  case value2:
```

```
        //code
        break;
    default:
        //default code
}
```

**Example**

```
<?php
$num = 20;
switch($num){
    case 10:
        echo "Number is equal to 10";
        break;
    case 20:
        echo "Number is equal to 20";
        break;
    default:
        echo "Invalid Number";
}
?>
```

Output

Number is equal to 20

- **Switch Statement with Character**

**Example**

```
<?php
$ch = 'U';
switch($ch){
    case 'A':
    case 'E':
    case 'I':
    case 'O':
    case 'U':
```

```
    echo "Given character is vowel";
    break;
  default:
    echo "Given character is consonant";
}
?>
```

**Output**

Given character is vowel

- **Switch Statement with String**

**Example**

```
<?php
$course = "B.Tech";
switch($course){
  case "BCA":
    echo "BCA is 3 years course";
    break;
  case "B.Tech":
    echo "B.Tech is 4 years course";
    break;
  default:
    echo "Wrong Choice";
}
?>
```

Output

B.Tech is 4 years course

- **PHP For Loop:** The for loop is used when the number of iterations is known.
- **Syntax**

```
for(initialization; condition; increment/decrement){
  //code
}
```

**Example**

```
<?php
for($n = 1; $n <= 10; $n++){
  echo "$n <br/>";
}
?>
```

Output

1

2

3

4

5

6

7

8

9

10

- **PHP Nested For Loop:** A for loop inside another for loop is called nested for loop.

**Example**

```
<?php
for($i=1; $i<=3; $i++){
  for($j=1; $j<=3; $j++){
echo "$i $j <br/>";
  }}
?>
```

Output

1 1

1 2

1 3

2 1

2 2

2 3

3 1

3 2

3 3

- **PHP Foreach Loop:** The foreach loop is used to traverse array elements.

**Syntax**

```
foreach($array as $value){
  //code
}
```

**Example**

```
<?php
$season = array("Summer","Winter","Spring","Autumn");
foreach($season as $arr){
  echo "Season is: $arr<br/>";
}
?>
```

Output

Season is: Summer

Season is: Winter

Season is: Spring

Season is: Autumn

- **PHP While Loop:** The while loop executes repeatedly until the condition becomes false.
- **Syntax**

```
while(condition){
  //code
}
```

**Example**

```
<?php
$n = 1;
while($n <= 10){
  echo "$n <br/>";
```

```
  $n++;
}
?>
```

Output

1

2

3

4

5

6

7

8

9

10

- **PHP Nested While Loop:** A while loop inside another while loop is called nested while loop.

**Example**

```
<?php
$i = 1;
while($i<= 3){
  $j = 1;
  while($j <= 3){
    echo "$i $j <br/>";
    $j++;
  }
  $i++;
}
?>
```

Output

1 1

1 2

1 3

2 1

2 2

2 3

3 1

3 2

3 3

- **PHP Do-While Loop:** The do-while loop executes at least once because the condition is checked after execution.
- **Syntax**

```
do{
  //code
}while(condition);
```

**Example**

```
<?php
$n = 1;
do{
  echo "$n <br/>";
  $n++;
}while($n <= 10);
?>
```

Output

1

2

3

4

5

6

7

8

9

10

- **PHP Break Statement:** The break statement terminates loop execution immediately.

**Example**

```
<?php
for($i=1; $i<=10; $i++){
  echo "$i<br/>";
  if($i == 5){
    break;
  }}
?>
```

Output

1

2

3

4

5

- **PHP Continue Statement:** The continue statement skips the current iteration and moves to the next iteration.

**Example**

```
<?php
for($i=1; $i<=10; $i++){
  if($i == 5){
    continue;
  }
  echo "$i<br/>";
}
?>
```

Output

1

2

3

4

6

7

8

9

10

## 6.4 Arrays

### PHP Arrays

PHP array is an ordered map that stores values based on keys. Arrays are used to hold multiple values of similar type in a single variable.

### Advantages of PHP Arrays

- **Less Code:** There is no need to create multiple variables for storing similar values.
- **Easy Traversal:** All elements of an array can be accessed using a single loop.
- **Sorting:** Array elements can be sorted easily using array functions.

### Types of PHP Arrays

PHP supports three types of arrays:

1. Indexed Array
2. Associative Array
3. Multidimensional Array

- **PHP Indexed Array:** Indexed arrays store elements with numeric indexes starting from 0.Indexed arrays can store numbers, strings, and objects.
- **Ways to Create Indexed Array**
- **First Method**

```
$season = array("summer","winter","spring","autumn");
```

- **Second Method**

```
$season[0] = "summer";
$season[1] = "winter";
$season[2] = "spring";
$season[3] = "autumn";
```

**Example**

```
<?php
$season = array("summer","winter","spring","autumn");
```

```
echo "Season are: $season[0], $season[1], $season[2] and $season[3]";
?>
```

Output

Season are: summer, winter, spring and autumn

Indexed Array using Second Method

```
<?php
$season[0] = "summer";
$season[1] = "winter";
$season[2] = "spring";
$season[3] = "autumn";
echo "Season are: $season[0], $season[1], $season[2] and $season[3]";
?>
```

Output

Season are: summer, winter, spring and autumn

### ▶ PHP Associative Array

Associative arrays store values using named keys instead of numeric indexes.The => operator is used to associate keys with values.

### ▶ Ways to Create Associative Array

### ▶ First Method

```
$salary = array(
  "Sonoo"=>"350000",
  "John"=>"450000",
  "Kartik"=>"200000"
);
```

### ▶ Second Method

```
$salary["Sonoo"] = "350000";
$salary["John"] = "450000";
$salary["Kartik"] = "200000";
```

### ▶ Example

```
<?php
$salary = array(
  "Sonoo"=>"350000",
  "John"=>"450000",
```

```
  "Kartik"=>"200000"
);
echo "Sonoo salary: ".$salary["Sonoo"]."<br/>";
echo "John salary: ".$salary["John"]."<br/>";
echo "Kartik salary: ".$salary["Kartik"]."<br/>";
?>
```

Output

Sonoo salary: 350000

John salary: 450000

Kartik salary: 200000

Associative Array using Second Method

```
<?php
$salary["Sonoo"] = "350000";
$salary["John"] = "450000";
$salary["Kartik"] = "200000";
echo "Sonoo salary: ".$salary["Sonoo"]."<br/>";
echo "John salary: ".$salary["John"]."<br/>";
echo "Kartik salary: ".$salary["Kartik"]."<br/>";
?>
```

Output

Sonoo salary: 350000

John salary: 450000

Kartik salary: 200000

### ▶ PHP Multidimensional Array

A multidimensional array is an array containing one or more arrays.

It is also called an array of arrays.

Multidimensional arrays are used to store tabular data in the form of rows and columns.

### ▶ Definition of Multidimensional Array

```
$emp = array(
  array(1,"sonoo",400000),
  array(2,"john",500000),
```

```
  array(3,"rahul",300000)
);
```

► **Example**

```
<?php
$emp = array(
  array(1,"sonoo",400000),
  array(2,"john",500000),
  array(3,"rahul",300000)
);
for($row = 0; $row < 3; $row++){
  for($col = 0; $col < 3; $col++){
    echo $emp[$row][$col]." ";
  }
  echo "<br/>";
}
?>
```

Output

1 sonoo 400000

2 john 500000

3 rahul 300000

► **PHP Array Functions:** PHP provides many built-in array functions to manipulate and access array elements.

**1) PHP array() Function**: The array() function creates and returns an array.

► **Syntax**

```
array array([ mixed $... ])
```

**Example**

```
<?php
$season = array("summer","winter","spring","autumn");
echo "Season are: $season[0], $season[1], $season[2] and $season[3]";
?>
```

Output

Season are: summer, winter, spring and autumn

**2) PHP array_change_key_case() Function**: This function changes the case of all keys in an array.It changes only the keys, not the values.

▶ **Syntax**

array array_change_key_case(array $array [, int $case = CASE_LOWER ])

**Example using CASE_UPPER**

```
<?php
$salary = array(
  "Sonoo"=>"550000",
  "Vimal"=>"250000",
  "Ratan"=>"200000"
);
print_r(array_change_key_case($salary, CASE_UPPER));
?>
```

Output

Array ( [SONOO] => 550000 [VIMAL] => 250000 [RATAN] => 200000 )

**Example using CASE_LOWER**

```
<?php
$salary = array(
  "Sonoo"=>"550000",
  "Vimal"=>"250000",
  "Ratan"=>"200000"
);
print_r(array_change_key_case($salary, CASE_LOWER));
?>
```

Output

Array ( [sonoo] => 550000 [vimal] => 250000 [ratan] => 200000 )

**3) PHP array_chunk() Function:** The array_chunk() function splits an array into smaller parts.

▶ **Syntax**

array array_chunk(array $array, int $size [, bool $preserve_keys = false ])

**Example**

```
<?php
$salary = array(
```

```
    "Sonoo"=>"550000",
    "Vimal"=>"250000",
    "Ratan"=>"200000"
);
print_r(array_chunk($salary,2));
?>
```

Output

```
Array (
[0] => Array ( [0] => 550000 [1] => 250000 )
[1] => Array ( [0] => 200000 )
)
```

**4) PHP count() Function**: The count() function counts the total number of elements in an array.

▶ **Syntax**

```
int count(mixed $array_or_countable)
```

**Example**

```
<?php
$season = array("summer","winter","spring","autumn");
echo count($season);
?>
```

Output

4

**5) PHP sort() Function:** The sort() function sorts array elements in ascending order.

▶ **Syntax**

```
bool sort(array &$array)
```

**Example**

```
<?php
$season = array("summer","winter","spring","autumn");
sort($season);
foreach($season as $s){
    echo "$s<br/>";
```

```
}
?>
```

Output

autumn

spring

summer

winter

**6) PHP array_reverse() Function:** This function returns array elements in reverse order.

▶ **Syntax**

array array_reverse(array $array)

**Example**

```
<?php
$season = array("summer","winter","spring","autumn");
$reverseseason = array_reverse($season);
foreach($reverseseason as $s){
  echo "$s<br/>";
}
?>
```

Output

autumn

spring

winter

summer

**7) PHP array_search() Function**: The array_search() function searches a value in an array and returns its key.

▶ **Syntax**

mixed array_search(mixed $needle, array $haystack)

**Example**

```
<?php
$season = array("summer","winter","spring","autumn");
$key = array_search("spring",$season);
```

```
echo $key;
?>
```

Output

2

**8) PHP array_intersect() Function:** The array_intersect() function returns common elements between arrays.

▶ **Syntax**

array array_intersect(array $array1, array $array2)

**Example**

```
<?php
$name1 = array("sonoo","john","vivek","smith");
$name2 = array("umesh","sonoo","kartik","smith");
$name3 = array_intersect($name1,$name2);
foreach($name3 as $n){
  echo "$n<br/>";
}
?>
```

Output

sonoo

smith

## 6.5 PHP String

PHP string is a sequence of characters used to store and manipulate text. PHP supports a 256-character set and does not provide native Unicode support.

PHP provides four ways to define strings:

1. Single Quoted String
2. Double Quoted String
3. Heredoc Syntax
4. Nowdoc Syntax

### Single Quoted String

A single quoted string is created by enclosing text within single quotes (' ').

It is the simplest way to define strings in PHP.

In single quoted strings:

- Variables are not interpreted.
- Most escape sequences are not interpreted.
- Only \' and \\ are recognized.

**Example 1: Single Quoted String**

```
<?php
$str = 'Hello text within single quote';
echo $str;
?>
```

Output

Hello text within single quote

**Example 2: Multi-line Text in Single Quotes**

```
<?php
$str1='Hello text
multiple line
text within single quoted string';
$str2='Using double "quote" directly inside single quoted string';
$str3='Using escape sequences \n in single quoted string';
echo "$str1 <br/> $str2 <br/> $str3";
?>
```

Output

Hello text multiple line text within single quoted string

Using double "quote" directly inside single quoted string

Using escape sequences \n in single quoted string

**Example 3: Variables and Escape Characters in Single Quotes**

```
<?php
$num1 = 10;
$str1 = 'trying variable $num1';
$str2 = 'trying backslash n and backslash t inside single quoted string \n \t';
$str3 = 'Using single quote \'my quote\' and \\backslash';
echo "$str1 <br/> $str2 <br/> $str3";
?>
```

Output

trying variable $num1

trying backslash n and backslash t inside single quoted string \n \t

Using single quote 'my quote' and \backslash

- **Important Note about Single Quotes**
  - Variables are not interpreted.
  - Escape sequences like \n and \t are printed as plain text.
  - Only \' and \\ work as escape sequences.

## Double Quoted String

A double quoted string is created by enclosing text within double quotes (" ").

In double quoted strings:

- Variables are interpreted.
- Escape sequences are interpreted.

### Example 1: Double Quoted String

```
<?php
$str = "Hello text within double quote";
echo $str;
?>
```

Output

Hello text within double quote

### Example 2: Invalid Use of Double Quotes

Double quotes cannot be used directly inside another double quoted string without escape character.

### Program

```
<?php
$str1 = "Using double "quote" directly inside double quoted string";
echo $str1;
?>
```

Output

Parse error: syntax error

### Example 3: Escape Sequences in Double Quotes

### Program

```
<?php
$str1 = "Hello text
```

```
multiple line
text within double quoted string";
$str2 = "Using double \"quote\" with backslash inside double quoted string";
$str3 = "Using escape sequences \n in double quoted string";
echo "$str1 <br/> $str2 <br/> $str3";
?>
```

Output

Hello text multiple line text within double quoted string

Using double "quote" with backslash inside double quoted string

Using escape sequences in double quoted string

**Example 4: Variable Interpretation in Double Quotes**

## Program

```
<?php
$num1 = 10;
echo "Number is: $num1";
?>
```

Output

Number is: 10

- PHP provides many built-in string functions to manipulate strings.

**1) PHP strtolower() Function:** The strtolower() function converts all characters into lowercase.

**Syntax**

```
string strtolower(string $string)
```

**Example**

```
<?php
$str = "My name is KIRAN";
$str = strtolower($str);
echo $str;
?>
```

Output

my name is kiran

**2) PHP strtoupper() Function:** The strtoupper() function converts all characters into uppercase.

**Syntax**

string strtoupper(string $string)

**Example**

```
<?php
$str = "My name is KHAN";
$str = strtoupper($str);
echo $str;
?>
```

Output

MY NAME IS KHAN

**3) PHP ucfirst() Function:** The ucfirst() function converts the first character of a string into uppercase.

**Syntax**

string ucfirst(string $str)

**Example**

```
<?php
$str = "my name iskIRAN";
$str = ucfirst($str);
echo $str;
?>
```

**Output**

My name is KIRAN

**4) PHP lcfirst() Function**: The lcfirst() function converts the first character of a string into lowercase.

**Syntax**

string lcfirst(string $str)

**Example**

```
<?php
$str = "MY name IS KIRAN";
$str = lcfirst($str);
echo $str;
?>
```

Output

mY name IS KIRAN

**5) PHP ucwords() Function:** The ucwords() function converts the first character of every word into uppercase.

**Syntax**

string ucwords(string $str)

**Example**

```
<?php
$str = "my name is Sonoo jaiswal";
$str = ucwords($str);
echo $str;
?>
```

Output

My Name Is Sonoo Jaiswal

**6) PHP strrev() Function:** The strrev() function reverses a string.

**Syntax**

string strrev(string $string)

**Example**

```
<?php
$str = "my name is Sonoo jaiswal";
$str = strrev($str);
echo $str;
?>
```

Output

lawsiajoonoSsiemanym

**7) PHP strlen() Function**: The strlen() function returns the length of a string.

**Syntax**

int strlen(string $string)

**Example**

```
<?php
$str = "my name is Sonoo jaiswal";
$str = strlen($str);
echo $str;
```

```
?>
```

Output

24

## 6.6 PHP Regular Expressions (Pattern Matching)

Regular Expressions are commonly known as **Regex**. A regular expression is a sequence of characters that defines a search pattern.

Regex is mainly used for:

- Searching patterns in strings
- Replacing text
- Splitting strings into parts
- Validating user input

Regular expressions use special symbols and operators to create patterns.

By default, regular expressions are case-sensitive.

### Advantages and Uses of Regular Expressions

**1. Text Validation:** Regex helps programmers validate text strings.

**2. Pattern Searching**: Regex provides powerful methods to search and analyze patterns inside strings.

**3. Pattern Modification:** Regex allows replacement and modification of text easily.

**4. HTML Tag Recognition:** Regex is useful in recognizing HTML tags while creating templates.

**5. Form Validation:** Regex is widely used for,

- Browser detection
- Form validation
- Spam filtering
- Password strength checking

**6. User Input Validation:** Regex helps validate Email addresses, Mobile numbersandIP addresses.

**7. Keyword Highlighting:** Regex helps highlight keywords in files or documents based on search results.

**8. Complex Pattern Creation:** Metacharacters allow creation of advanced search patterns.

#### ▶ PHP Regex Example

```
<?php
//initialize a variable of string type
```

```
$website = "JTP is a best online platform to learn.";
//case insensitive search for word jtp
$res = preg_match('/jtp/i', $website, $matches);
if($res){
  echo "Pattern matched in string.</br>";
print_r($matches);
}
else{
  echo "Pattern not matched in string.";
}
?>
```

Output

Pattern matched in string.

Array ( [0] => JTP )

## 6.7 PHP Form Handling

PHP forms are used to collect user input.

PHP uses superglobal variables to retrieve form data:

- $_GET
- $_POST

The form request can be either:

1. GET Method
2. POST Method

▶ **PHP GET Form:** GET is the default request method.

### Features of GET Method

- Data is visible in URL.
- Less secure.
- Limited amount of data can be sent.

### Example of GET Form

**File: form1.html**

```
<form action="welcome.php" method="get">
Name: <input type="text" name="name"/>
<input type="submit" value="visit"/>
</form>
```

**File: welcome.php**

```
<?php
$name = $_GET["name"];
echo "Welcome, $name";
?>
```

- **PHP POST Form:** POST method is used for sending large and sensitive data.

## Features of POST Method

- Data is not visible in URL.
- More secure than GET.
- Large amount of data can be sent.

## Example of POST Form

**File: form1.html**

```
<form action="login.php" method="post">
<table>
<tr>
<td>Name:</td>
<td><input type="text" name="name"/></td>
</tr>
<tr>
<td>Password:</td>
<td><input type="password" name="password"/></td>
</tr>
<tr>
<td colspan="2">
<input type="submit" value="login"/>
</td>
</tr>
</table>
</form>
```

**File: login.php**

```
<?php
$name = $_POST["name"];
```

```
$password = $_POST["password"];
echo "Welcome: $name, your password is: $password";
?>
```

### ▶ PHP Include and Require

PHP provides file inclusion concepts to reuse code in multiple pages.

Two methods are available:

1. include
2. require

## Advantages of Include and Require

- **Code Reusability:** HTML and PHP code can be reused in multiple files.
- **Easy Maintenance:** Editing one source file automatically updates all pages using it.

### ▶ PHP include

The include statement inserts content of one file into another file.

If file is missing, include generates a warning but execution continues.

### ▶ Syntax of include

```
include 'filename';
OR
include('filename');
```

### ▶ Example of include

**File: menu.html**

```
<a href="http://www.javatpoint.com">Home</a> |
<a href="http://www.javatpoint.com/php-tutorial">PHP</a> |
<a href="http://www.javatpoint.com/java-tutorial">Java</a> |
<a href="http://www.javatpoint.com/html-tutorial">HTML</a>
```

**File: include1.php**

```
<?php include("menu.html"); ?>
<h1>This is Main Page</h1>
```

### ▶ PHP require

The require statement is similar to include.

If the file is missing, require stops script execution with a fatal error.

- **Syntax of require**

```
require 'filename';
OR
require('filename');
```

**Example of require**

**File: require1.php**

```
<?php require("menu.html"); ?>
<h1>This is Main Page</h1>
```

## 6.8 PHP Cookie

A cookie is a small piece of information stored in the user's browser.

Cookies help identify users.

- **PHP setcookie() Function:** The setcookie() function creates cookies.
- **Syntax**

```
setcookie("CookieName", "CookieValue");
setcookie("CookieName", "CookieValue", time()+1*60*60);
```

- **Example of Cookie**

```
<?php
setcookie("user", "Sonoo");
?>
<html>
<body>
<?php
if(!isset($_COOKIE["user"])){
  echo "Sorry, cookie is not found!";
}
else{
  echo "<br/>Cookie Value: " . $_COOKIE["user"];
}
?>
</body>
</html>
```

**Output**

Cookie Value: Sonoo

- **Delete Cookie:** Cookies can be deleted by setting expiration time in the past.

**Example**

```
<?php
setcookie("CookieName", "", time() - 3600);
?>
```

## 6.9 PHP Session

A PHP session stores user information temporarily across multiple pages.

Sessions are widely used in:

- Shopping carts
- Login systems
- User authentication

- **PHP session_start() Function:** The session_start() function starts or resumes a session.

- **Syntax**

```
session_start();
```

- **PHP $_SESSION**

$_SESSION is an associative array used to store session variables.

- **Store Session Data:** $_SESSION["user"] = "Sachin";
- **Access Session Data:** echo $_SESSION["user"];

- **Session Example**

**File: session1.php**

```
<?php
session_start();
$_SESSION["user"] = "Sachin";
echo "Session information are set successfully.";
?>
<a href="session2.php">Visit next page</a>
```

**File: session2.php**

```
<?php
session_start();
echo "User is: ".$_SESSION["user"];
?>
```

### ▶ Destroy Session

The session_destroy() function destroys all session data.

**Example**

```
<?php
session_start();
session_destroy();
?>
```

## 6.10 PHP File Handling

PHP provides functions to:

- Create files
- Read files
- Write files
- Delete files
- Close files

▶ **PHP fopen() Function:** The fopen() function opens a file.

**Syntax**

```
fopen(filename, mode);
```

**Example**

```
<?php
$handle = fopen("c:\\folder\\file.txt", "r");
?>
```

▶ **PHP fclose() Function:** The fclose() function closes a file.

**Example**

```
<?php
fclose($handle);
?>
```

▶ **PHP fread() Function:** The fread() function reads file content.

**Example**

```
<?php
$filename = "c:\\myfile.txt";
$handle = fopen($filename, "r");
$contents = fread($handle, filesize($filename));
```

```
echo $contents;
fclose($handle);
?>
```

- **PHP fwrite() Function:** The fwrite() function writes data into a file.

**Example**

```
<?php
$fp = fopen('data.txt', 'w');
fwrite($fp, 'hello ');
fwrite($fp, 'php file');
fclose($fp);
echo "File written successfully";
?>
```

- **PHP unlink() Function:** The unlink() function deletes a file.

**Example**

```
<?php
unlink('data.txt');
echo "File deleted successfully";
?>
```

## 6.11 PHP MySQL Database Operations

PHP provides MySQLi functions to interact with databases.

Operations include:

- Create Database
- Create Table
- Insert Record
- Update Record
- Delete Record
- Select Record

- **PHP MySQL Create Database**

**Example**

```
<?php
$conn = mysqli_connect("localhost:3306","","");
$sql = "CREATE DATABASE mydb";
```

```
if(mysqli_query($conn,$sql)){
  echo "Database created successfully";
}
?>
```

- **PHP MySQL Create Table**

**Example**

```
<?php
$conn = mysqli_connect("localhost:3306","","","test");
$sql = "CREATE TABLE emp5(
id INT AUTO_INCREMENT,
name VARCHAR(20) NOT NULL,
emp_salary INT NOT NULL,
PRIMARY KEY(id)
)";
mysqli_query($conn,$sql);
?>
```

- **PHP MySQL Insert Record**

**Example**

```
<?php
$conn = mysqli_connect("localhost:3306","","","test");
$sql = 'INSERT INTO emp4(name,salary)
VALUES("sonoo",9000)';
mysqli_query($conn,$sql);
?>
```

- **PHP MySQL Update Record**

**Example**

```
<?php
$conn = mysqli_connect("localhost:3306","","","test");
$sql = "UPDATE emp4
SET name='Rahul', salary=80000
WHERE id=2";
mysqli_query($conn,$sql);
?>
```

## ▶ PHP MySQL Delete Record

**Example**

```
<?php
$conn = mysqli_connect("localhost:3306","","","test");
$sql = "DELETE FROM emp4 WHERE id=2";
mysqli_query($conn,$sql);
?>
```

## ▶ PHP MySQL Select Record

**Example**

```
<?php
$conn = mysqli_connect("localhost:3306","","","test");
$sql = "SELECT * FROM emp4";
$result = mysqli_query($conn,$sql);
while($row = mysqli_fetch_assoc($result)){
  echo "EMP ID : ".$row['id']."<br>";
  echo "EMP NAME : ".$row['name']."<br>";
  echo "EMP SALARY : ".$row['salary']."<br>";
}
?>
```

www.ingramcontent.com/pod-product-compliance
Lightning Source LLC
LaVergne TN
LVHW010725061126
851857LV00014B/1339
* 9 7 8 9 3 4 8 6 4 2 0 5 9 *